After many years working as a chef in Sydney, Jane Lawson moved into publishing, combining her love of travel, cooking and books. She is the author of *Snowflakes and Schnapps*, *Spice Market*, *Grub*, *Yoshoku*, *A Little Taste of Japan*, *Cocina Nueva*, *Zenbu Zen* and 2016's *Milkbar Memories*.

Jane is also the co-author of *BBQ Food for Friends*, which won a Gourmand World Cookbook Award in 2003.

Jane has been travelling around Japan for over thirty years. She runs independent tours to Japan on a regular basis, guiding her clients to the best that the country has to offer, from culture to fashion, food and lifestyle. Her particular area of interest is Japanese cuisine.

Visit zenbutours.com for more information.

TOKYO
STYLE GUIDE

eat * sleep * shop

TOKYO

STYLE GUIDE

JANE LAWSON

MURDOCH BOOKS
SYDNEY · LONDON

Tokyo

Nippori
10

Kappabashi
Yanesen 10
8
Kichijoji   Nakano   Korakuen   Okachimachi
6   6   9   8 Asakusa
6   7   9
Koenji   Kagurazaka   7   9   9 Kuramae
                                    9 Akihabara
Harajuku   Kanda-Ochanomizu
Shimokitazawa 3   1
                        2 Aoyama
Daikanyama   4   1
                        Shibuya
Naka Meguro 4
                5
                Ebisu
        5
Meguro

CONTENTS

INTRODUCTION

Before you embark on your Tokyo journey, allow me to paint you a picture. While the greater Tokyo Megalopolis is home to a rather daunting 37-plus million people—earning Tokyo the title of most densely populated 'urban area' in the world—this guide's focus is solely upon the core of the city region, with its relatively comfortable 'daytime' population of around 11 million.

Cosmopolitan Tokyo is a city built for discovery. Surprises, from the dizzying to the delightful, wait around every corner, every day—and that is what makes this place so exciting. And at times exhausting!

The intensely beating heart of Tokyo Metropolis is comprised of twenty-three special wards—each presenting and running as individual cities themselves. They are connected by a complex and overwhelming system of above- and underground railways. While this arrangement appears to be as tangled as weeds, it is a completely efficient and effective way to traverse the sometimes-confusing city terrain.

Conveniently, surrounding most of the close to 200 train stations are hundreds, sometimes thousands of shops, restaurants, bars and other services catering to the busy, hungry commuter hoards.

With the 2020 Tokyo Olympics looming, businesses are opening and closing and precincts are morphing and growing at such an untrackable pace that should you not visit a particular area for six months, it may well be rendered almost unrecognisable upon your return. Most Tokyoites I've spoken to about this find it just as incredible as it sounds to you and me.

For this very reason, any travel dialogue claiming to be the 'quintessential guide to Tokyo' should probably be avoided. As a local shopkeeper grumbled to me, 'People who closely follow the standard Tokyo guidebooks inevitably end up becoming extremely frustrated.'

My aim in this particular guide is merely to give you a sense of place and style for certain pockets of Tokyo that I like to wander— for a variety of reasons. Some days I desire to be in the thick of it, soaked in youthful vigour and neon dreams. At other times I prefer the slower, more relaxed pace of a beautiful garden stroll, a lingering cuppa or sitting quietly in a lesser-known museum space.

I've included some of my favourite places, which I hope stand the test of time for your visit. If a certain shop or restaurant is no more, something just as interesting or delicious has probably taken its place.

This guide is specific where it needs to be and free and flowing when it is over to you to truly drive your own experiences. While I've included some counterpoints and well-considered suggested routes to follow, you will absolutely find your own magic along the way—trust me. Getting lost in Tokyo is to be expected, so take a deep breath and make it part of the fun. You are never far from one of those train stations, or a taxi, if you need to wing your way back to a particular start or end point.

The key to staying sane in a town of this magnitude is to go with the flow. The Japanese are masters at it—watch them move in the streets in what would be a mosh-pit crush elsewhere, or wait patiently at an overcrowded station stuck to their neighbours on all sides like glutinous rice—it is as though they stand peacefully alone with their thoughts.

It is impossible to go hungry or suffer design, art, coffee or shopping withdrawal, or fatigue, in any part of ever-changing Tokyo. Brace yourself for a special kind of culture shock and dive on in.

GENERAL TOKYO TRAVEL TIPS

WHAT TO WEAR

You'll quickly notice that the Japanese are rather snappy dressers and, even at their most relaxed, almost always immaculately groomed. So, when you plan your travel wardrobe, bear that in mind in order to feel less self-conscious.

As a general rule, middle-aged local folk (and in Japan that's anyone over thirty!) dress elegantly—either on the conservative or artsy side of the fashion line.

If you lean towards black, darker colours or natural tones, you will fit right in with the mainstream crowd. But in this city of contrasts, no one will bat an eyelid at a fluoro jacket with leopard-print pants outside Central Business District (CBD) areas. If you are attending meetings, you will need to dress conservatively. However, if you are merely here for a good time, think smart casual for day and a little more dressy for special restaurants or outings.

Plunging necklines and itsy-bitsy summer shorts might look fantastic on you, but may draw unwanted attention in Japan. Leave the ripped jeans, singlet tops and thongs (flip-flops) at home—unless you plan to spend your entire trip hanging out in grungier parts of town, with the young and hip who don't give a fig about conformity. At least until they find themselves working in an office job.

In temples you are expected to act and dress respectfully.

A note on footwear

Wear supportive, comfortable shoes or boots for days you'll be walking a lot, and bring a nice pair for evenings if you are dining out. Make sure your shoes slip or zip on and off easily, as you will be required to remove them for visits to most traditional buildings, such as temples and shrines, and people's homes. Certain businesses, such as restaurants and some shops, and anywhere there is tatami, will also require you to remove your shoes. So do make sure you take newish, hole-free socks to avoid embarrassment.

THE SEASONS

J apan experiences four distinct seasons (and twenty-four mini-seasons but that's a story for another day …). While Tokyo, being close to the east coast, suffers fewer extremes than inland parts of Japan, it's still helpful to be prepared.

Winter/Fuyu (Dec–Feb) is cold but pales in comparison to most of Europe and the colder parts of America. Yes, you will need a warm coat, gloves, scarves, socks and comfortable footwear, preferably boots, for walking. It rarely snows to the point of ground cover. If it does snow heavily enough to achieve a frosty white wonderland effect, it usually disappears within a couple of days. Mostly the days are clear and blue-skied and, for me, it's the perfect weather for wandering—then warming up in a cosy café when you need a break. There are fewer tourists in winter, which makes getting around easier than busier times of year. Average temperature range: 0–12ºC (32–54ºF)

Spring/Haru (Mar–May) presents beautiful, even-keeled weather with ample blooms, which are both stunning and responsible for the overwhelming crowds. Sakura (cherry blossom) time in late March/early April means every Tokyoite and tourist is getting amongst it—picnics in the park, a stroll by the river and selfie-stick sword fights. Book accommodation and fancy restaurants well ahead of time. A smart cardigan or light jacket will be necessary on most days, and in early spring you'll absolutely need something warmer for evening. Average temperature range: 5–22ºC (41–72ºF)

Summer/Natsu (Jun–Aug) is, to be frank, generally hot and humid, and sometimes rather rainy. However, it is a time of festivals and fun—particularly in the evenings. Dress as light as possible but keep it neat and respectable, especially if you are visiting temples. You'll be amazed how the Japanese seem to keep their cool on the hottest days. Summer is my least favourite time to visit Japan, but I am drawn to frostier climes and reach melting point at 28ºC (82ºF). If you have opposite tastes with regard to this you will probably love it! Average temperature range: 19–31ºC (66–88ºF)

Autumn/Aki (Sept–Nov) days, like those in spring, are relatively even-keeled. Relief from the heat combined with the stunning rust, red and gold-hued gardens draws squillions of locals out from the air-conditioning in early autumn. It's a popular tourist season, so booking trains and accommodation early is good idea. September can still be quite warm but by November things have cooled down considerably and the air is crisp. For me, autumn is an attractive time to visit Japan. The blossoms of spring are truly pretty—and need to be seen just once in your life—but they are fleeting, whereas the autumn leaves make their transition over a longer period, and to witness the gradual shading, even over a week, can be magical. Average temperature range: 10–25ºC (50–77ºF)

GETTING FROM A TO B

In a nutshell, **trains** run like clockwork in Japan and are generally the fastest, most reliable and economical way to access all areas of Tokyo Town. **www.jreast.co.jp/e/**

However, buying a ticket on the right line for the perfect station for your destination, when you have thousands of people suddenly queuing behind you eager not to miss their ride, may send even the most rational of folk into a state of anxiety.

To save you a lot of grief, I highly recommend purchasing a **Suica or Pasmo card**. You top them up as needed and away you go. They are available at most large train stations and suitable for most lines. Occasionally, a smaller private line might require you buy a ticket. Look for the ticketing office or a vending machine.

If you do purchase a ticket and have accidentally underpaid, there is no issue; simply use the fare adjustment machines, which are available at most stations before you enter the turnstiles. Otherwise, show a staff member your ticket at the ticket gate.

To make the most of your precious travel time, use the excellent **Hyperdia** search engine to research your route before you set out. It not only tells you how to get to and from your destination but also provides departure times, length of journey, how much it costs and where you need to change stations and lines. **hyperdia.com/en/**

If you are going to a venue not mentioned in this guide, check their website for specific exit numbers. Some stations are enormous and have many exits that can take you far away from where you wish to go if you're not prepared.

I suggest you occasionally take a **taxi** in order to fit everything into your day or to simply rest your feet! Note: taxi doors open and close automatically, and don't sit in the front seat unless you absolutely have to—taxi drivers prefer that customers sit in the back.

DIRECTIONS

The address system in Japan can at times be mind-boggling. Locals talk about the north/south/east/west sides of the street when giving directions—often with a description of how far it is from a particular building or monument. I've done this where I can to make things easier.

BUSINESS OPENING HOURS

Shops generally open from around 10 or 11 am through to 7 or 8 pm. However, these operating hours are not across the board. Convenience stores operate longer hours and offer international ATMs.

Days of closure for businesses in Tokyo are determined by the individual business or facilities. Check the website of any venue you really want to visit to make sure it's open when you get there. It is reasonably common that a business has a weekday off—often Tuesday or Wednesday—rather than closing on a weekend when sales peak.

Restaurants commonly start serving lunch around 11 am and finish around 2 pm. If you don't have a reservation, it pays to arrive as close to opening as possible. Dinner service starts around 5.30 pm and many casual places close quite early too. Check individual websites for details.

POSTAL SERVICES

Buy and post home! Japan has an affordable and efficient postal service. Hotels can sometimes arrange this for you, or go to the post office with your goods. They have boxes and paperwork, and you are good to go once a fee is paid—it is surprisingly good value and safe. You'll also find international ATMs at post offices.

MOBILE PHONES

That's right, your all-important phone. Although you may be able to rely on it at home, it's important to note that your own phone may or may not work on Japan's telecommunications network. Even it if does manage to tap in, you'll be forking out a small fortune in roaming fees.

While some may be happy to live in a cone of silence while on leave, I prefer to carry a mobile phone. Let's set aside the convenience of checking email and answering calls on the run when you are travelling for business. I use it to find a certain venue and to access GPS mapping systems, such as Google maps, which are a tremendous assistance in a city where it is too easy to lose your way. I highly recommend you use a digital map service with GPS with this book.

Instead of using my own phone I rent one with an unlimited data package and a cheap international call rate. I always rent the same brand as my own for ease of use and to link to all my apps and contacts. It has saved me on many occasions and besides, how would I flood Instagram with Japan images without it? I've found **Global Advanced Communications** to be the most reliable vendor. **globaladvancedcomm.com/**

BASIC COMMUNICATION

Let's assume you don't speak a word of Japanese. I'll come right out and say that it is highly likely you'll find some aspects of travelling in Japan a little difficult. While the Japanese do learn English as part of the school curriculum, they are usually a little reticent to use it for fear of embarrassment or miscommunication. However, it never hurts to try. Keep your language simple. Gestures are your friend.

There has traditionally been little signposted in English, but with the impending Olympic-traveller traffic there is a steady increase in English signage across Tokyo. This will make a huge difference to your stay. Still, there will be times when it helps to have a few basic phrases up your sleeve and the ability to recognise a couple of important Japanese-language characters.

Whenever you enter a business, shop or restaurant, or even on the street if someone smiles at you, it is considered polite to at least be able to say hello! But there are three ways to say it depending on the time of day.

Greetings
Good morning—from early morning until around 11 am.
Ohayoo gozaimasu
Pronounced 'ohio' like the state; 'goz-eye-mus' as in mustard.

Good day— After 11 am and before 5 pm.
Konnichiwa
Pronounced like 'con–itchy–wa', with the 'a' sound like the 'u' in 'up'.

Good evening—after 5 pm.
Kombanwa
Pronounced like 'com' as in 'combination', 'bun' as in 'pork bun', and 'wa' as above.

Goodbyes
Sayonara
Pronounced 'sigh', 'yon' as in 'on', 'a' as in 'up', and 'ra' as in 'run'.

To say goodbye at night, when leaving a venue or going to bed
Oyasuminasai
Pronounced 'o' as in 'on', 'ya' as in 'yuk', 'sumi' like 'sue me!' but with a shorter 'u' sound, 'na' as in 'nup', 'sigh'.

Giving thanks

It is much appreciated if you can say 'thank you' in Japanese whenever someone does something for you. There are several ways to say it, depending on the level of thanks you are giving, and your relationship to, or the status of, the person you are giving it to, but to make it easy just go with these two variations.

Thanks!

Arigatou
Pronounced 'a' like the 'u' in 'up', 'ri' as in 'rip', 'ga' as in 'gut', 'tou' sounds like the word 'saw' but with a 't'—'taw'.

Thank you so much—slightly more formal
Arigatou gozaimasu
The 'arigatou' pronounced as above and the second word: 'goz-eye-mus' as in 'mustard'.

Please

Please in its most basic form (and also the easiest to pronounce).
O kudasai
Pronounced 'o' as in 'often', 'ku' as in 'cook', 'da' as in 'darling', and 'sigh'. For example, if you wanted someone to pass you a pen you'd say "pen o kudasai."

Please when closer to meaning 'could you please do that', or 'please, would that be okay'? Can be used as a 'yes please' for when someone offers to do something for you.
Onegai shimasu
Pronounced 'o' as in 'often', 'ne' as in 'never', 'gai' like 'guy' but with a soft 'ng' sound to begin, 'shi' like 'shivers', 'mus' as in mustard. For example, if someone asks if you would like a receipt/glass of water etc., a slight nod or bow with an 'onegai shimasu' is a polite way to say, 'yes, please, would you mind?' It is a little hard to pronounce at first but listen to the way people say it around you, and you'll soon get the drift.

Yes or no?

In Japan, it is better to stick to 'yes' as much as possible. Avoid the negative and perhaps overly direct 'no' unless you really have no other choice. Gently shaking your head or hands with a 'sumimasen' or 'gomenasai' ('excuse me' or 'I'm sorry') will get you out of most situations where you feel the need to decline. If it's an emergency or you can't think of any other word to say 'no', then go for it.

Yes
Hai
Pronounced as in 'high' but with a shorter, sharper 'i' sound.

No
Iie
Sounds like 'ee' as in 'we' and 'e' as in 'pet'.

Excuse me and I'm sorry!

When you want to get someone's attention—be it a waiter in a restaurant, a shop attendant or simply when trying to get past someone who is in your way—there is a very useful word that works as both 'excuse me, I need your attention' and 'I'm sorry'. For example, in the case where you bump into someone accidentally—and you will! Wait and see—everyone uses it and you should too. It's also sometimes used as a way to break the silence before speaking to someone generally.

The magic word is:

Sumimasen
Pronounced 'su' as in 'sue' but with a shorter 'u' sound, 'mi' as in 'mini', 'mus' like 'mustard', and 'en' as in 'end'.

However, there is another word that simply means you are genuinely sorry, as in 'I'm sorry I spilt my water on the table', 'I'm sorry I did the wrong thing', 'I'm sorry to hear that sad news'.

That is:

Gomenasai

Pronounced 'go' as in 'got', 'men' not women, 'a' as in 'up', 'sigh'.

When nature calls

You will probably need to ask where the 'conveniences' are at some point in your stay. (Tip: Department and convenience stores!)

Where is the toilet?

Toire wa doko desu ka

Pronounced 'toy', 're' like 'red', 'wa' with 'a' sounding like the 'u' in 'up', 'do' as in 'dog', 'ko' as in 'cod', 'desk', 'a' like the 'u' sound in 'up'.

Someone will point you in the general direction, or may go out of their way to show you to the entrance—don't take that as creepy, the Japanese generally place more importance on helping out a foreigner in need and sometimes go to the extreme.

If you manage to locate the bathroom on your own, it is helpful to know the Japanese characters for 'Male' and 'Female' just in case there are no obvious icons on the door.

(Otoko) Male   (Onna) Female

Entrance and exit

You'll find many large shops or places to visit, such as museums, temples and gardens, have dedicated entrance and exit signs. They often have roped-off areas for queuing—a necessary tool in a country so heavily populated, and where people respond well to ordered spaces and events. No queue jumpers in this civilised society, so you'll want to know how to get in and out without causing a fuss.

(Iriguchi) Entrance   (Deguchi) Exit

HARAJUKU
& SHIBUYA

KEY

This precinct can be bold, brash and busier than you can probably imagine, but with that comes colour, the addictive energy of a pre-teen and much frivolity. Youngsters and tourists are drawn here like starving ants to a jam sandwich. The shopping is great if you are seeking the latest international fashions, and it is certainly a place to see and be seen—particularly on the weekends.

On one level, it isn't as cutting edge as it used to be—the more grungy, earthy and eclectic types have moved to suburbs such as Koenji (p153) or nearby Shimokitazawa (p76)—but it is still fun to people-watch. It recently became the first ward in Tokyo to recognise gay marriage, so I'd suggest a shift towards more boutique, homegrown-style offerings is in the wings for the future. But right now, at first glance, it feels far more Americanised than other parts of Tokyo. So, if name brands and American culture appeal, look no further.

Regardless of your personal style, the area is an absolute must-see for any first-time visitor—you really can't get more quintessentially Tokyo than this! Conveniently, you can easily step across into sophisticated Aoyama (p52) from many Harajuku streets that connect, and at times confuse themselves, with their neighbour.

Shibuya is most famously photographed for its eternally busy five-way pedestrian crossing. While I sometimes go out of my way to avoid this crazy-busy part of town, when I am face to face with it I am at least consistent in my excitement while I wait for the change of crossing lights. I often stay to experience and photograph several ordered human-tsunamis before I step off the kerb myself.

The entire area is an entertainment hub predominantly ruled by shopping, eating and drinking. It is best bitten off in small chunks if you have time, as it can be quite overwhelming in an audiovisual sense. Below I share a mere overview—if you like what you see, come back again and focus on the parts you found most compelling. Shibuya is currently under heavy construction leading up to the Olympics in 2020, when it will likely resemble a scene from *Blade Runner* even more closely than it does now.

Close to **Harajuku Station** 🌐 and the majestic **Meiji Jingu (shrine)** ➊, 'kids' still dress up and perform in **Yoyogi Koen (park)** ➋ on the weekends. Rockabillies, punks, lolitas, goths and closet cosplayers clump together in a curious, slightly rebellious cultural display—if only for the day. When the bustling flea market is in full swing, the place is even more jumping than usual. Like most markets (p291), it is a great place to pick up the kinds of souvenirs you don't see in regular retail establishments.

SUGGESTED WALK

L et's start at **Harajuku Station** 🌐. Follow the throng of over-excited teens as you exit onto street level in front of the quaint old station house. Turn right (south) and walk for a few moments until you see a wide pedestrian bridge over the tracks on your right. It's a popular meeting place, so it is likely to be busy with foot traffic. Over the bridge and to your right you will find the start of the towering tree-lined path to the **Meiji Jingu (shrine)** ➊ through the first enormous wooden torii gate. I find a brief cultural visit has a calming effect on me before I throw myself into the crowds of Harajuku. Founded in 1920 to commemorate the beloved Emperor

Meiji and his wife after their consecutive passing a few years earlier, this is one of the largest and most popular shrines in Tokyo, situated at the heart of a sacred forest of trees donated in their honour. It can be busy on the weekends but is spacious enough to handle the masses. The shrine commonly hosts traditional wedding ceremonies, so keep your eyes peeled for the most magnificent costumes and processions —sometimes you can sneak a peek at the formal ritual itself.

When you exit the shrine, veer right and venture into **Yoyogi Koen (park)** ❷. There's something exciting happening here most weekends—from monthly antiques markets to full-tilt festivals to dance troupes, rock bands and pretty young things (PYTs) flouncing their frilliest outfits just because—did someone say photo op? Look out for the plural Elvis! Elvi? They've been around for the last couple of decades and don't appear to be going anywhere soon. Things don't get seriously jumping until late morning. If the markets are in full swing you can't miss them—there's likely to be a thousand or so people milling around the stalls at any given time. If you are into street food, you'll find stalls selling okonomiyaki, yakisoba and takoyaki—popular snacks—although the quality is hit and miss.

When you've had your fill of buskers' competing tunes and circus acrobatics, head back over the footbridge, cross at the lights and walk down the hill with **Harajuku Station** ❺ on your left side until you come to a colourful archway on your right: the entrance to **Takeshita Street** ❸. The unfathomably busy laneway before you is lined with youth-engaging fashion outlets, from vaudeville-punk to saccharine kawaii (Japanese for cute), burger joints, accessory stores and sweet crepe stands.

Brace yourself and keep pushing forwards but do make sure you take in the entertaining scene. If you have small kids, hold them close lest they be swept away in the people sea. Teenage girls? Tell them you'll meet them at the other end in a couple of hours—there will be no stopping them from wildly diving in and out of the cutesy fashion and curio outlets and you, my stylish friend, might be better off finding a gorgeous café.

The east exit of Takeshita Street delivers you to Meiji Dori —cross at the lights and you are at the entrance to Harajuku Dori. Continue east along this lane into a slightly less frantic part of Harajuku known as Urahara (backstreet Harajuku) where the fashions become a little more interesting and varied, and a more eclectic range of goods starts to appear in the many tiny stores.

The skinny streets around here are rather captivating. If you were to head in the direction of Aoyama, (continuing east on Harajuku Dori) the crowd thins for a while and you'll find yourself in a residential area dotted with more stylish offerings for slightly more mature, creative tastes (*see* Aoyama chapter for more details p52).

However, focusing back on where Harajuku Dori meets the famous **Cat Street** ❹—a long street running parallel to and just east of Meiji Dori)—turn right (south) just after the Family Mart convenience store. Here, the café options start to open up, tucked in neatly between designer camping and sports gear, handmade jewellery and Americana fashions.

When you hit Omotesando Dori, a wide boulevard linking Harajuku to Aoyama, lined with high-end fashions and mixed goods, turn left and walk up the gently sloping street towards the **Omotesando Hills** ❺ shopping complex on your left—officially

④ ⑤

on the edge of Aoyama. The centre itself is architecturally captivating, with more tilts and levels than a pinball machine. There's certainly a bunch of high-end shopping to be had, but also many handsome dining options and one elegant sake-tasting bar. One of the more casual offerings is **Golden Brown** ❻, an excellent burger joint and the perfect lunch stop for engaging with some of your own youthful nostalgia—if you can't beat 'em join 'em—but rest assured there's no mucking about with the menu. Serious burger action and great fries. Wash it down with a beer or soda. Keep an eye out for Japan's own Wilkinson's Ginger Ale by Asahi in two strengths—the 'Dry' is delightfully spicy.

After you're done shopping and eating, leave the centre, walk a little further up the road to the next crossing (near the Apple store) and take it to access the opposite side of Omotesando Dori. Double back now on that side of the street towards the part of Cat Street

that continues south of Omotesando. Along the way, almost cowering under the shadows of taller neighbouring buildings with brilliant glass facades such as Coach, Hugo Boss, Louis Vuitton and Dior, you'll find the ever-popular **Oriental Bazaar** ❼. If you have just one day in Tokyo and have a souvenir order list for everyone—from babies to your mother-in-law to your sister's boyfriend's dachshund—this is the place to find the kind of items you'd anticipate, from the terribly obvious to the rather lovely: kimono, traditional and modern tableware, sushi, T-shirts, Mount Fuji replicas, antiques and ninja outfits.

Just after Oriental Bazaar, I recommend going to the **Gyre Building** ❽ for a quick walkthrough, making sure to stop at the **MoMA store** ❾—they have a very succinct selection of Japanese design goods, including ceramics, glassware, jewellery, books, quirky knick-knacks and stationery items. In the basement food hall you'll find a range of fancy takeaway food, including an outlet of New York's famous **Magnolia Bakery** ❿. Grab a to-die-for pecan brownie to take back to your hotel room … I did mention the area's predilection for all things American?

It is best bitten off in small chunks if you have time, as it can be quite overwhelming in an audiovisual sense.

Before you skip down the remaining part of Cat Street, take a peek into the children's paradise going by the name of **Kiddy Land** ⓫ —the five-storey Harajuku flagship toy shop first opened over sixty years ago. Try to go when it is quiet or risk being trapped at the back of the 'sushi-rice-packed' store by juvenile shoppers. Games, hobbies, dolls, characters, stationery, decorations—you name it—if it's cutesy or cool (in a primary-school child kinda way) they have it!

Backtrack slightly to enter Cat Street on your right (south). As you walk towards the Shibuya end, you'll notice several quality second-hand designer and vintage clothing stores. In the evening, this area becomes quite lively thanks to restaurants, bars and cafés in adjacent streets. If you have time, take some of the side alleys and explore— returning to the main vein after each distraction. The fun and quirky window displays along this street make it worth a stroll whether you are purchasing or not!

Don't miss **Quico** ⑫—a cool interiors, tableware and 'wardrobe' store arranged with head-turning fabrics, bowls, woven bamboo baskets, designer furniture and the like—by turning left off Cat Street between the Columbia and Oakley stores. If you turn right at this same junction, you'll find lots of sweet little boutiques, jewellery stores and cafés along the winding alleyways.

About halfway between Omotesando and the Shibuya end of Cat Street, you'll find **The Roastery by Nozy Coffee** ⑬—a happy example of when Tokyo does coffee well and the roasting is done in situ. Tokyo's coffee scene is a relatively new one and you can rest assured that their single-origin brews are a far cry from the burning-tyre-flavoured mud from yesteryear's kissaten (old-fashioned coffee shops). Amen, coffee gods. Don't get me wrong—I love a good kissaten for the atmosphere—and these days many have switched their coffee game to 'on'! Do keep an eye out for one in the quieter areas—it is a particularly charming time-warping experience. I highly recommend resting weary feet now and recharging for an evening in Shibuya. And if it's 'that time of the day', a Coffee 'Porter' beer makes an excellent kickstarter.

… you'll find lots of sweet little boutiques, jewellery stores and cafés along the winding alleyways.

A little further down the street on the same side of the road is the Ocean Tokyo Building. Venture inside and underneath the Suzu Café (a great place to people-watch if you can get a window seat!), is **Scrapbook (Jeanasis)** ⑭—think Genesis, 'original goods'. The white, concrete-grey and blonde-wood industrial interior is the perfect blank palette for a mix of original Japanese design goods, from clothing, trainers, accessories and make-up to stationery and a tiny but well-curated book selection.

Continuing in the same direction, you'll pass Shibuya High School and before you reach the next Family Mart Conbini (convenience store) you'll arrive at **C-Plus Head Wares** ⑮—a tiny yet well-stocked treasure chest of spiffy caps, berets, hats and beanies. A few buildings later, just before the ultra-quirky, giant-golden-egg-adorned **Pink Dragon** ⑯ (aka Rock and Roll Department)—a 1950s copycat apparel and nostalgia store, complete with secret dragon museum

inside and serviced by suitably coiffed rockabilly types—you'll note the end of Cat Street.

Follow the road as it veers slightly left onto Meiji Dori and keep walking towards Shibuya Station for about four blocks until you reach a main intersection—you'll have just passed the huge **BIC Camera Store** ⑰ on your right. If you are in the market for extra photographic or computer gear during your travels, this is a well-kitted-out mega-store with competitive prices.

Facing BIC Camera Store, cross at the lights at the corner just south of the store so that you are heading west. Within minutes you'll arrive at the aforementioned **five-way crossing** ⑱. But pay careful attention here because before you get that far, there's a special, albeit nondescript laneway that travels along the right side of the Yamanote line train tracks. If evening is nigh you'll see a lantern-lit alleyway—this is **Nonbei Yokocho** ⑲ (loosely translating as 'drunkards' alley').

Head directly into it for a delightfully gritty time-shift away from modern Shibuya.

Two parallel alleyways host a number of shack-like tiny bars and eating spaces with just a handful of seats in each, yet these are home to a host of incredible characters—both the shopkeepers and customers. You can bounce between them tapas style, nibbling on yakitori or home-style dishes—or get intimate with the barman over a Hibiki Hiball. A stand-out joint, and particularly popular late-night bar within the local community, is the glowing **Red Bar ⑳** (aka chandelier bar, open in the evening). If you can squeeze your way up the stairs you'll have earned yourself a drink or two at this fabulous mini bar. The crowd is an eclectic mix of handsome young things and grungier, wizened, creative types with whom you can't help but become engaged, as you will pretty much be sitting on each other's laps.

The crowd is an eclectic mix of handsome young things and grungier, wizened, creative types ...

Once sated, head back to the main road and keep walking just a few minutes more towards the **Shibuya Station** area, which hosts an incredible number of shopping centres, including the hard-to-miss Shibuya 109 building with its several-storeys high, illuminated advertising. **Shibuya 109 ㉑** is a landmark that assures you've landed in the right place, so look up if you think you are lost. Between Shibuya 109 and the JR (Japan Railways) Hachiko entrance to the station is a paved area, home to a relatively small statue of a famous dog, of the same name. The dog was immortalised for his loyalty—waiting nightly by the station gates for his master to return home, even years after his passing. Hachiko demonstrates the kind of perseverance revered by the Japanese and is consequentially a popular meeting place, which promises to be so crowded that you can barely find the poor dog.

Now I'm not a shopping centre kinda gal—to enter one tends to make my blood run cold, and if you feel the same way you might not wish to spend too much time shopping in this particular section of town. However, if you are tempted to sample just one, I'd recommend you cross through the station and exit on the eastern

side. In fact, there's a walkway above the road that links to a newish office skyscraper, containing a shopping mall called **Hikarie 22**. It has a much better layout than most; the stylish stores within it feel like individual offerings. There are also several comfortable restaurants if the bar alley seemed a bit daunting—and if you head up to the higher floors, where there is often an interesting cultural or creative event taking place, you have an impressive birds-eye view over greater Shibuya.

Retrace your steps back across to **Shibuya Station** and depart from there. ●

KEY

The atmosphere of Aoyama on a sunny, blue-skied Sunday is one of unencumbered vacation joy—if your idea of the perfect break involves relaxed shopping, eating, sipping quality coffee and people-watching. There's more than enough material to fill a stylish postcard or two here.

Lining the main belt of Aoyama Dori are luxury goods and haute couture fashions from across the globe—often showcased in spectacular, glittering architectural triumphs—interjected with elegant restaurants and cafés for appropriate 'glamour day' shopping pit stops.

The flashiest sports cars lazily crawl the streets seeking attention, and the uber-yen'd step out with their primped twin toy poodles in matching outfits. However, if your origami-folding wallet isn't lined with gold leaf, you'll be happy to learn that tucked into the back streets of Kita (north) and Minami (south) Aoyama—running along and behind both sides of the main street—are a range of spunky smaller boutiques, design-driven homewares, traditional goods and a more casual class of restaurant and café.

Aoyama (Blue Mountain), offers a more sophisticated experience than its neighbours Harajuku and Shibuya (p28)—both within winking distance. There are enough shopping and pampering opportunities in Aoyama to pack a good weekend, but if you've got your skates on and possess enough self-control to just window-shop, you can traverse the entire area in a day.

1

SUGGESTED WALK

Exit **Omotesando Station** ⊖ onto Aoyama Dori. There are several exits but look for B4, which will pop you out near the corner of Aoyama Dori and the peak of the Omotesando Dori slope (connecting you to Harajuku in the furthest part of the street).

If you are visiting on a weekend or public holiday, the **farmers' market at the United Nations University (UNU)** ❶ will be in full swing by 10 am, so head about 400 metres along Aoyama Dori in the direction of Shibuya. You are now on the edge of Shibuya, just south of what is known as Kita Aoyama. You could easily dawdle around the market for an hour discovering new ingredients, organic products or the odd antique, and meeting smiley farmer types. If you're staying in an apartment in Tokyo, it's not a bad place to stock the kitchenette.

Retrace your steps just a few metres north of the market, where **Pierre Hermé ❷** promises to alleviate any serious macaron and chocolate withdrawal a traveller may be suffering. Although that would be unlikely given that Tokyo caters for even the most insatiable sweet tooth.

Just moments further north, your roving eye for style will inevitably spot a **Found Muji ❸** store on your left. While most of us know and love megabrand Muji for its commitment to making well-priced, stylish and functional lifestyle products, we can now also enjoy a range of gorgeous, hand-selected Muji 'findings' from Japan and around the world—an ever-changing and eclectic collection of homewares, including cookware and linen, decorative items and clothing—all in keeping with their pricing philosophy.

Continue on to the mesmerising glass AO building, and if exquisitely handmade Japanese jeans of uncompromising quality

are on your shopping list, make sure you pop in to **Momotaro Jeans ❹**. Japanese denim, dyed with natural indigo, has become a hot-ticket item in recent years and deservedly so, with the high-level craftsmanship that goes into making them, but there's also a selection of complementary apparel and accessories. There's not a lot else to see in the building, except some fine eateries. I highly recommend returning to **Two Rooms ❺** (p278) for dinner if you are still in the area at the end of the day.

Unless you have plans to drop your annual mortgage payments on a diamond necklace, cross Omotesando Dori when you reach it and pop your blinkers on. Continue north about 300 metres past a variety of high-end stores and all too many fur-parents exercising their freshly pampered pooches. After you pass the palatial Brooks Brothers, take the next laneway on your left, at the Aoyama Takano building. Down here you'll stumble on **OPA gallery shop ❻**.

This is a cool, fun store of regularly changing showpieces handmade by local creatives.

Once you're back out on the street, keep walking west until you come to a second intersection. Now you've hit the main artery of a maze of laneways that link this part of Aoyama to Harajuku's Cat Street (p36), Urahara further west, and Omotesando Dori to the south. There is a great vibe here—a good mix of folk from the neatly dressed and well heeled to bo-ho/hipster types and young, cutting-edge fashionistas.

You'll no doubt be ready to continue moving after your fill of porky goodness—but if you head home for a nap no one will blame you.

Should you choose to turn right here, you'll pass several great places for coffee and something light to eat—including the popular **Bread and Espresso ❼** and **Lattest Omotesando Espresso Bar ❽**.

However, if you are hoping to try some of Japan's famous tonkatsu (fried, breaded pork cutlet) then head left, past the healthier options at **Mr. FARMER ❾**—an organic café using produce from small local farms in salads, soups and sandwiches—to the honten (main shop) of the famous **Maisen ❿**. Go for the top-of-the-line offerings by arriving early if you can—lunch in Japan starts around 11 am! If you like the sweetness and tender texture of fatty pork, you should snap up one of the limited number of rosu katsu (sirloin) specials on offer, at the counter, before the locals beat you to it. There's ebi furai (fried prawns) with tartare sauce and crab croquettes for the non-meat eaters. If the queue is extra long, and it often is, there are katsu-sando (sandwiches) at a kiosk at the front. You'll no doubt be ready to continue moving after your fill of porky goodness—but if you head home for a nap no one will blame you.

If you are up for venturing into Harajuku (p28), take the next right and you'll be in a street that runs all the way down to Cat Street. The area between is mainly residential, with some interesting homes to lust over—from sleek, cutting-edge architectural designs of polished concrete and coloured glass in natural hues to beautifully restored traditional houses. A few shops and cafés are dotted about.

Taking us back a step to **Maisen ❿**, travel about seven buildings south and on the left is charming **Gallery Kawano ⓫**, specialising

in antique kimono and textiles. This well-organised store sells second-hand kimono, yukata (lightweight summer kimono), obi (kimono sashes), and fabric offcuts in a kaleidoscope of colours. Staff are friendly and speak enough English to be helpful with sizing and coordinating colours and patterns.

Directly ahead is a T-junction. If you take a right you will end up back down near Cat Street and Omotesando Dori, only you'll find a few more shops on this particular route.

If continuing on with the tour, take a left. The back of Gold's Gym will be on your right, above the strategically placed Afternoon Tea Tea Stand and See's Candies on your left. Also on your left will be **nest Robe ⓬**, which sells elegant-casual Japanese fashions for both women and men in natural tones and fabrics. Much of the ladieswear is size F for 'free' and flowy—and great for travel.

Take the next right and walk until you hit Omotesando Dori. Cross at the lights near the Apple store on your left and continue straight, via the long lane between the Coach and Hugo Boss stores.

Now if you skipped the tonkatsu because you were looking for something a little more 'clean', take a step to the right and check out **Brown Rice Canteen** ⑬ at Neal's Yard. Their very affordable set lunch containing tofu and seasonal vegetables will cleanse your body and mind of any shopper's guilt.

Follow this street all the way along. It is dotted with some fine fashions and old-school, European-looking homes, so if you're interested in some of the more curious architecture statements in these parts, take some time to explore. This is another of those streets that snakes all the way to Harajuku (p28) if you head west, then Shibuya (p28) to the south.

Keeping on our route, take a left at the T-junction. **Shito Hisayo** ⑭ will be on your right—showcasing the designer's alluringly contemporary (and expensive) kimono—and just past that you'll come to **Daimonji** ⑮. This impressive store houses a varied selection of ceramics, lacquerware and glass vessels for the table and home at reasonable prices. I can't leave this place without at least a sublime little sake cup to add to my collection.

Take the next right and walk to the end of the lane. Here is the Aoyama outlet of France's **APC** ⑯—an upmarket, smart-casual apparel store in a handsome building that drops down from street level. Above it are not one, but two excellent Japanese incense stores. **Shoyeido** ⑰ —traditional, handcrafted incense from Kyoto, established in 1705 and of extremely high quality—and **Lisn** ⑱, their modern offshoot, in a far more glamorously kitted-out shop next door, touting delicate sticks in fashion colours and scents with enticing names conveniently printed on each length. The sample collections, which change with every season, are extremely gift-worthy—even if said gift is for self. I adore the incense from both establishments but the packaging and accoutrement (burners and containers) at Lisn appeal to a style-conscious audience. Japanese incense is not cloying like it can be from other countries, and burning it back at home will ensure you sustain holiday memories of Japanese temples and Zen hummings.

H ead out eastward to Aoyama Dori and you'll be back on the corner at **Found Muji** ❸. Turn left and cross the road at the next set of lights. You are now in Minami (South) Aoyama, a section running southeast of Aoyama Dori. There's a slightly different vibe from the other side of Aoyama Dori in this precinct, even though it's just metres away, and it's just as lovely to stroll around in.

If you turn right, you'll see the handsome and innovative lifestyle concept store **Bloom & Branch** ⑲. Here, you will find newer Japanese artisan goods and antique folkcraft, plus a selection of quality wearables from clothing to jewellery. There's also a small café hidden inside. Right next door is **Tsutaya** ⑳, selling tea ceremony accoutrements—beautiful tea canisters and the like—and handcrafted tools for ikebana (traditional flower arrangement). Cross the road (north) and take the laneway that runs behind Max Mara, parallel to Aoyama Dori. Explore the small laneways that run off this

有松 窯
白瓷織部小鉢
税込 ¥3,888
(本体 ¥3,600)
一客

有松 窯
織部丸小皿
税込 ¥3,672
¥3,400

貫入小鉢
税込 ¥2,160
(本体 ¥2,000)
一客

織部つわぶき皿
税込 ¥2,700
(本体 ¥2,500)
一客

15

17

21

24

long lane or simply follow your path all the way to the northern end. Along the way you'll pass **Madu** ㉑—definitely worth a gander for more excellent Japanese homewares—and a wide variety of places to eat and drink. At the opposite end of the spectrum is a beautiful, traditional Japanese confectionery (wagashi) store called **Higashiya** ㉒.

If you turn right just before Higashiya you'll be in a dazzling part of Aoyama, which particularly twinkles in the early evening—showing off sumptuous window displays for the likes of Comme des Garçons, Chloé and Cartier, and the majestic rhomboid of diamond-shaped glass and metal that Prada calls home. Walk as far as **Plain People** ㉓ for the kind of original and extremely covetable clothing and goods you don't see every day, with occasional lifestyle goods pop-ups, too.

There's an ancient tea house at its heart, and lots of shady nooks to sit and ponder ...

Just a little further in this direction is the delightful **Nezu Museum** ㉔. Famous not only for its vast private collection of pre-modern Japanese (and other Asian) art, including tea ceremony ceramics, calligraphy scrolls, textiles, bamboo craft and sculptures—but also for its lush green stroll garden, which is worth a visit alone. There's an ancient tea house at its heart, and lots of shady nooks to sit and ponder the jizo and other deities that line your path. The café is in a sleek, modern Zen-inspired setting with large viewing windows to drink in the peaceful greenery. It feels so very far from the heart of Aoyama, it's as if you've slipped away for a mini-break. I highly recommend interjecting a visit into your shop-hopping Aoyama day.

The National Art Centre ㉕ is just a short taxi-ride from here. The centre is spectacular beyond belief. The building, designed by internationally acclaimed architect Kisho Kurokawa, is precisely how you might imagine an apex experience in a Tokyo avant-garde art scene. I'd go there to gaze into its awesome steel and glass construction even if there weren't a drop of art within its shell. In fact, the National Art Centre has no permanent collection or curators of its own. It is obvious, even to an amateur art appreciator like myself, how much consideration is given to ensure the viewing experience

of each exhibition is a deeply emotional and perfectly timed affair. Each collection has its own fresh perspective and energy. From the immaculate brushstrokes of a master calligrapher to the breathtakingly raw beauty of works from immerging Japanese artists, the focus is on diversity and connection. The dining facilities range from simple café to top-notch gourmet, allowing you to spend as much time lingering in this stupendous space as possible. Don't miss the basement museum shop, **Souvenir from Tokyo** ㉖—almost a separate exhibition space of desirable art and design products.

Returning to **Higashiya** ㉒ for now … beyond it, at the end of the road heading north, turn left, and on your right is the famous **Blue Bottle** ㉗ coffee from America—aimed to impress serious coffee aficionados. The highly revered California-based roaster has just two outlets in Japan—both in Tokyo—one with a roastery attached. The

spacious Aoyama café includes a patio area and specialises in drip-style, espresso and iced coffee alongside sweet and savoury pastries.

If something a little stronger is due to wet your whistle, take the next right into the side entrance of **Commune 246** ㉘ where a camp of food vans and stalls is set up, with little tables for relaxing with your takeaway. The atmosphere is jovial, and it's not a bad way to end the day and rest those hard-working feet.

However, if it's dinner o'clock by the time you've finished denting your credit card and you're looking for an equally fabulous and glam experience to match the day you've just had, I recommend you head back to **Two Rooms** ❺—in the AO building. ●

SHIMOKITAZAWA

Shimokitazawa

SHIBUYA &
HARAJUKU →

Odakyu Odawara Line

Keio Inokashira Line

Shimokitazawa
Station

NAKA MEGURO
↓

It's hard to put your finger on it, but there's something rather appealing about the less stitched-up, not-so-perfectly gleaming nature of Shimokitazawa. It is understandably popular with artists and musicians but it is also reported to be one of the most desirable Tokyo villages to live in among young folk generally. There are many casual, well-priced eateries here, and caffeine addicts are properly catered for.

It's easy to forget how close you are to the hustle-bustle of Shibuya when in the small, laid-back town of Shimokitazawa—or 'Shimokita' in the local lingo. The first thing you notice is how pleasantly relaxed and friendly the shopkeepers seem to be, followed by the palpable sense of fun. While there are a couple of big-name local stores in this low-rise suburb—Muji, for example—most shops are independently owned, which has helped to develop the area's layered personality.

Street art comes in the form of happy and colourful graffitied shop shutters—cleverly tempting you to return in the opening hours for what lies beyond.

Things don't get moving until a little later in these parts. It's a youthful, slightly grungy neighbourhood reeking of arts-college city campus—in a good way. With that comes shedloads of vintage and retro fashions, antique goods and used records at reasonable prices. Plus a range of places in which to be entertained on various levels. Save exploring Shimokitazawa for a lazy day.

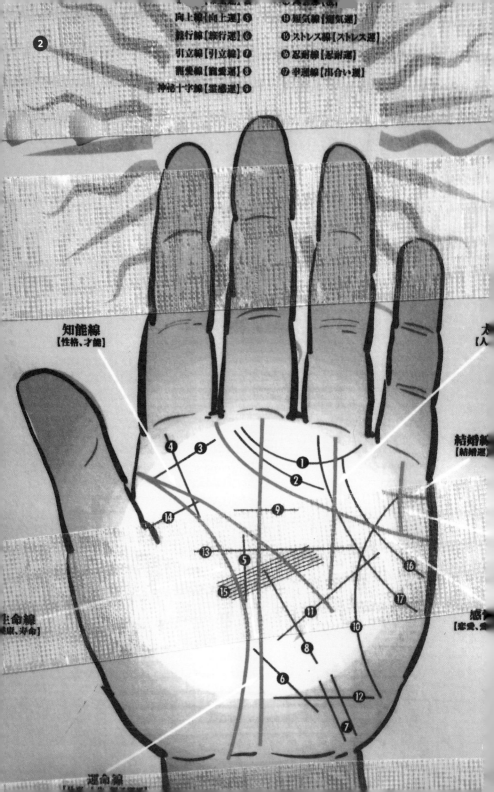

② 向上線【向上運】⑤　　　⑭短気線【短気運】
　　旅行線【旅行運】⑥　　　⑮ストレス線【ストレス運】
　　引立線【引立運】⑦　　　⑯忍耐線【忍耐運】
　　寵愛線【寵愛運】⑧　　　⑰幸運線【巡合い運】
　　神秘十字線【霊感運】⑨

知能線
【性格、才能】

恋人

結婚線
【結婚運】

生命線
【健康、寿命】

感
【恋愛、

運命線

SUGGESTED WALK

L ocate the northern gate at the east end of **Keio Shimokitazawa Station ⑤**. If you look left up the hill to your left, you'll spot megastore Muji, but right in front of you is a Mizuho bank. Walk around it so it's on your left. Directly ahead is one of several shopping strips in this compact maze of streets where new and vintage fashion boutiques huddle together with antiques and bric-a-brac, second-hand record stores and more hairdressers than seem necessary. Don't be surprised when you are regularly tricked by salons masquerading as fab cafés—there's a phenomenal number of them lying in wait throughout Tokyo.

Take a right about 100 metres ahead, just after the Sundrug store, and you are in a small section of **Ichibangai ❶**—a shopping strip catering to locals' daily needs since the 1920s. Take the next left at the Senbei (rice cracker shop) to continue on Ichibangai for all the essentials, such as fortune-telling café **Sencha ❷**, where a Japanese psychic reads your palm (take a translator!)—it's that kinda town.

Although the slender streets on the north side of the station cover a relatively small area, they are jam-packed and you could easily spend half a day here just mooching around. Any ordered navigation will surely end up in confusion and frustration, but just to get you started, take the next left after Sencha into the heart of **Ichibangai ❶** —a long, wider street that runs mostly north and a little south from this point, fairly parallel to the Keio station area. Go forth and investigate the cluster of shops, cafés and eateries running between the two—covering an area of about ten small blocks.

Trust me, you'll get your bearings once you've roamed past the same place twice. However, don't forget that getting giddy Tokyo-style is a lot of fun if you allow it. To give you some markers, I've noted a few points of interest on the map.

While many of the **apparel and accessories** stores appeal to a sub-thirty age group, do keep a lookout for the following: **Slick mist ❸**; **Marble Sud ❹** (also cleverly curated trinkets and curios [zakka]); **Soffitto ❺**; **Natural Laundry ❻**; **Pinkertons ❼**; **Ruelle ❽** (shares space with sibling store Barns and sports creative Japanese designs on denim for the menfolk; the manbags look fairly unisex to me!).

For **antique/vintage/retro** furniture, knick-knacks, clothing, toys, signage, homewares and the like, look out for **Antique Life Jin ❾**; **Alaska vintage clothing ❿**; **Flamingo ⓫**; **The Sun Goes Down ⓬**.

There are also a few excellent pop-up stalls that offer a mix of Japanese and international antiquities and preloved clothes, trinkets and interior items—worth a search through other people's trash to find the odd bit of treasure.

Shimokitazawa Garage Department ⓭ is home to an eclectic collection of tiny stores selling vintage clothing and handmade craft and design goods.

Kidults will be mesmerised by **B-Side Label** ⑭, one of the more curiously addictive stores selling only manga/anime-inspired stickers, badges and stationery by a collective of young Japanese designers. With these fun, vibrant, sometimes provocative images and quotes, you can end up wasting more time than you'd imagine here, giggling as you source some uniquely Japanese souvenirs. While expensive for stickers, they're also long-lasting, with UV protection so they don't fade. The store suggests personalising belongings, such as phone cases, tablets, laptops, bikes and skateboards, as a stamp of individuality—and in a country with so many people, it helps to have some identifying features on common goods.

You can end up wasting more time than you'd imagine, giggling as you source some uniquely Japanese souvenirs.

Shimokitazawa is well catered for with a significant range of reasonably priced 'ethnic' eateries—curry houses, Mexican, burgers and sandwiches seem to dominate. In fact, curry is so popular here they host an annual curry festival each October. There are also many Japanese options including soba, ramen and—in the evening—numerous izakaya and a few higher-end places serving more creative fare.

For excellent coffee, make your way to the tiny and uber-cool **Bear Pond Espresso** ⑮. The owner is a rock star of the Tokyo coffee scene.

If you need something sweet to go with your caffeine, pop directly across the street to the pretty **N.Y. Cupcakes Cupcakery** ⑯. The Japanese don't traditionally eat and drink while walking as it's considered bad manners, so find yourself a spot in the sun and relax.

If a cup of tea is more your thing, **8 Jours** ⑰ is a cutesy tea shop/café just up the road. Politely ignore the occasional cat motif and you'll be rewarded with a proper black tea or one of many specialty frou-frou tea drinks. And if you are hungry, they do a few savoury lunch items—quiche, baguette, croque monsieur, alongside sweet tarts and pancakes.

On the opposite side of the station (through the south exit) you'll find a larger area packing in loads more shops and eateries in a jumble of even more confusing laneways. You'll spy McDonald's ahead.

Walk down the street to its left-hand side. Just after the Sumitomo Bank you'll come to **Tenmaya Curry Pan** ⑱. Now, if you aren't hungry for one of Japan's favourite tasty snacks, do make a mental note for later, as you'll be missing out if you don't grab some of their famous stuffed fried-bread dough (think savoury donut) to snack on back in your room. They come filled with delectable curry, including butter chicken as well as the usual Japanese-style curries. My favourite has a perfectly gooey soft-boiled egg in the centre.

Now that crucial piece of information is out of the way you are free to roam the 'south side'. The retail offerings here do tend to be a bit more commercial than north of the station. However, there are still sufficient curio stores and second-hand goods, such as records and books, to please those seeking something less mainstream.

Return to McDonald's and walk south, so its shopface is now on your left. You'll be on one of the main arteries for shops and eateries (another runs parallel to and east of this street)—with smaller lanes branching off in all directions. Take a punt on the tucked-away alleys, where things are always bound to be a little more interesting.

Do be sure to seek out **Antiquaille** ⑲, a tiny, twenty-five-year-old antique shop crammed with all kinds of fascinating tins, toys, glassware, jewellery, ceramic cups and just about anything you can imagine. Lots of fun—when there are less than three customers!

Ideally, your schedule for Shimokita involves shopping on the south side in the late part of the afternoon, after a few hours perusing the north side. Then, you'd stay into the evening for drinks in an atmospheric, low-key bar or a 'live house' with, as the name would indicate, live music and a young, curious crowd.

The area celebrates a theatre culture, with a focus on the avant-garde, and retains a few old theatres in a cluster easy to locate from the **Shimokitazawa Station** Ⓢ south exit. If you keep walking past **Tenmaya Curry Pan** ⑱ down to the main road and take a left, you'll find the area just a few minutes past the Kitazawa Community Branch office and Disk Union store. Here, sandwiched between **Suzunari** ⑳, the theatre that started it all, and **Theater 711** ㉑, you'll find the rustic and atmospheric **Suzunari Yokocho** ㉒, home to numerous izakaya cheap eats. If you don't speak any Japanese, the theatre offerings might be a little difficult to decipher, but regardless, you'll be visually mesmerised—and the izakaya are bound to provide some colourful entertainment of their own.

Small as this town is, you'll realise once you arrive how easy it is to lose your direction, as the streets wind and cross in completely confusing patterns. So go with an open mind, don't try to fight it— just follow your nose. Some helpful soul will be happy to point out the direction of the station or, more likely, walk you back themselves!

If you are short on Tokyo time and wish to combine your Shimokita strolling with a charming cultural experience, take a 7-minute taxi ride to the nearby **Mingei-kan** ㉓ (folkcraft museum). In a quiet suburb infrequently visited by foreign tourists, inside an impressive Showa-era (1926–89) building, is an excellent private collection of folkcraft articles, including ceramics, lacquerware, bold calligraphy scrolls and tactile, organic textiles. The building itself, fronted by pretty plum trees, is worth the entrance fee alone. There is basic information in English. Keep an eye open for the regular exhibitions. ●

DAIKANYAMA & NAKA MEGURO

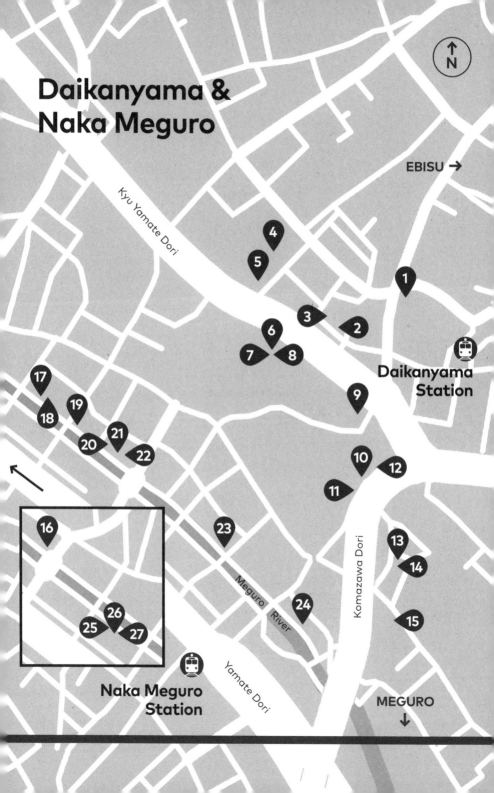

KEY

Daikanyama is a sophisticated pocket catering to the more moneyed, fashion-conscious crew with time on their hands for lingering lunches. It is dotted with delectable homewares, eye-catching threads and one of the best bookstores in Tokyo. Let's call it book nirvana for those interested in design, style and creative pursuits.

The Naka Meguro valley end of the Daikanyama slope is a little grungier and more indicative of how the entire area originally developed as a shopping destination—alternative fashions, relaxed cafés and curio outlets.

Neighbouring the greater suburb of Meguro, **Naka Meguro** is home to a small, hip enclave of predominately fashion stores and eateries running either side of a slender section of the Meguro River—near Naka Meguro Station.

Naka Meguro tends to wake up a little later in the day than many parts of Tokyo, making it the perfect spot for grabbing a weekend brunch and slowly shop-dawdling (after a late-night bar-hop in nearby Ebisu p110 perhaps?). Plan a light and breezy, take-your-time kind of day, where at least one meal spent lingering over a few cocktails forms an integral part of your agenda.

SUGGESTED WALK

For this duo of suburbs I prefer to begin the day in Daikanyama before it gets too busy, then make my way down the hill, ending in Naka Meguro. You can, of course, make it work either way if you'd rather a more 'uptown' dining experience in the evening—but keep in mind that most of the shops in Naka Meguro don't open till around 12 pm.

Turn right out of the north exit of **Daikanyama Station** Ⓜ and take the first street on your left. At the top of the street is a main road with a set of traffic lights and a towering lime-green flower sculpture. To your right are several fashion-focused shops, Francophile cafés and the once trendy but now slightly dated Daikanyama Address.

If you turn left, you'll start to see even more fashionable outlets, some with incredibly fancy-looking facades. For those who wear size S, lucky you! Knock yourselves out shopping the length of this street—and make sure you don't miss the laneways running off each side of the main road. Of course, if you'd prefer to follow me, I'll show you a few of my area favourites.

Turn left, away from the lime-green flower, and directly on your left is the **TENOHA & Style** complex ❶. This relatively new addition to the Daikanyama scene features '**& Style**'—a homogeneous blend of elegant Japanese garden and homewares, accessories and eco-conscious design products—with its own internal restaurant/café. It's the type of business you could do a figure-eight in for a couple of hours as you spot yet another gorgeous item you didn't notice the first time round because you were too distracted. They have some

truly beautiful table trinkets. And a spot of tea between circuits is a great way to extend your experience.

Once back outside, cross at the lights to the street directly ahead that leads northwest—take just a couple of steps to your right to enter it once you've exited the crossing. Here you will find a small but interesting collection of shops and cafés to amble in and out of on both sides of the strip. Also explore the laneways that run off to your left connecting to the parallel main road. You'll find books, chocolates, international fashion labels, records, handbags, delightful kids' outfits, shoes, beauty services and the ruggedly handsome **Hollywood Ranch Market** ❷ and **Rawlife** ❸—both for hip and sometimes quirky casual wear.

Walk through the 'garden' past **Ivy Place** ❹ on your right—a sprawling dining establishment—until you reach the rear garden entrance to the **Daikanyama T-site** ❺—the brainchild of the Tsutaya Bookstore chain.

If you are as loved-up with books as I am, you will be ecstatic simply losing yourself in this fantastic T-site store for hours.

If you are as loved-up with books as I am, you will be ecstatic simply losing yourself in this fantastic T-site store for hours. Not only does it have one of the most extensive and spectacular selections of beautiful, interesting and inspiring books and eclectic local and international magazines and periodicals—but it also has lots of cool, well-designed stationery and gifty bibs and bobs craftily dotted around the store relating to each genre. It is such a clever concept and an excellent assistance in putting together gifts for bookish friends. An extensive DVD and music selection is also on offer for those less inclined to purchase weighty books as souvenirs of their travels.

There are a couple of cafés within the shop itself, including the ubiquitous Starbucks, and a relaxed lounge area to linger over your purchases. While you are here, you might as well fully immerse yourself in the experience by lunching at **Ivy Place** ❹, but be sure to book ahead—it is huge, with a range of handsome dining spaces, including a cheery, sunlit glasshouse-like area, and it is always

packed! The food is touted as at-home-style dining, and features simple, flavoursome 'comfort' dishes, such as grilled meats and seafood, pasta, pizza, sandwiches and gourmet salads, served by glamorous staff in a venue that also acts as a premium perch for people-watching. Word on the street is that it is THE place to breakfast, and it's one of very few restaurants in Tokyo open from 7 am! Take heed, brunch fans!

Depart from the front exit onto Kyu Yamate Dori. Turn right to find a few more exclusive, conservative fashions and eateries. Cross the street at the next set of lights then turn left, walking back in the direction you came from. You are now in the vicinity of several international consulates—a fairly good indicator of the local clientele in these parts.

You'll pass even more shops and cafés before arriving at **Hillside Terrace ❻**, which does in fact stretch across to the other side of the

street but this is the main section. Pop in to **Makié Home** ❼ for sophisticated, coordinated fashions, accessories and homewares, and the shop's relaxing leafy perspective. **Greeniche** ❽ is a small store brimming with blonde-wood Scandi furniture and homewares, which are much coveted for modern Japanese apartments. You'll soon discover there's a comfortable and encouraged marriage between Japanese and Scandinavian design.

For a cultural pit stop, I highly recommend you turn right off the main road at the next street, just after **Hillside Terrace** ❻. Directly on your right is **Kyu Asakura House** ❾, built in 1919 by a local politician and chairperson of the Tokyo Council. The beautifully preserved traditional building is considered an important cultural property. Take some time to slowly slip in and out of each room with its tatami floors and sliding screen walls (shoji)—before taking the stepping-stones through the stroll garden, which is filled with

stone lanterns, azaleas and maple trees. The perfect respite. Seats are helpfully dotted around so you can take the weight off your feet, breathe and imagine another time. I like to plan where I'd put my furniture if they'd only let me move in.

Return to the main road and take a right to walk past the police box (koban), under the pedestrian overpass. Continue down the hill and turn right when you reach the corner. Just past here is a cute homewares/fashion store and coffee stand called **Life's** ❿. Just after that is **Hokodo Bijutsu** ⓫, an unassuming antiques shop filled to the brim with exquisite and somewhat expensive objects, including a significant collection of handcrafted tea bowls and other original tea ceremony accoutrements.

17

bulle de savon

bulle de sa

20

ACTS

You can either walk straight ahead, all the way down to Naka Meguro—you'll know it when you hit the river with decorative iron fencing—or you can take a more 'scenic' (aka shopping) route. To do so, retrace your steps just a few metres up the road to designer denim specialist **Evisu the Tokyo** ⓬ and cross the street.

You are now on Komazawa Dori. Turn right and walk down the hill about 50 metres, or until you see an orange wall to your left advertising Autobac. Turn left here. You'll see the Studio Daikanyama building in front of you where the road splits—walk past it so it is on your left and continue down this street. You'll come to a handful of eclectic bespoke and vintage fashion and goods stores, galleries and bars. Keep an eye out for **H** ⓭ by Jumpin Jap Flash Vintage and **Have a Good Time** ⓮.

There's a funkier, more creative vibe in these parts, only moments away from the more elegant and westernised Daikanyama stores. When you get to the bottom of the hill, take a quick left, past the Family Mart convenience store (always a good marker) to **Brick & Mortar** ⓯—an interior style goods store, which stages regular pop-up events with cool homewares designers or artists.

Take a left out of Brick & Mortar—continuing straight ahead through the tunnel with the pretty murals that runs under Komazawa Dori. Then take the next left and walk straight to the edge of Meguro River.

You are now at the epicentre of Naka Meguro, where you can really kick back. Proud green trees line the river along both sides, providing visual and mental refreshment. They offer cool shade in the warmer months and beauty in spring when the cherry blossoms embrace their short but exquisite lives.

I suggest you follow the row of attractive stores on each side, darting into the little alleyways for a peek at some of the tucked-away gems that occasionally pop up. There are some great independent businesses here specialising in fresh-faced, young, sophisticated fashions and homeware designs—often combined under the banner of lifestyle concept store—plus a few small chain boutiques.

My tips for this side of the river are as follows: **Snobbish babies** ⓰ (upmarket canine clothes and comfy clothes for their humans to walk them in); **bulle de savon** ⓱; **Red Clover** ⓲; **Carlife** ⓳; **ACTS** ⓴; **Hosu** ㉑; **Telepathy Route** ㉒; **Ouvrage Classe** ㉓; **Jean Nassaus Hale o Pua** ㉔.

Take a wander to the other side of the bridge and check out: **Leah-K** 25 (vintage specialist); **Kapuki** 26 (for exquisite contemporary kimono, yukata [summer kimono] and obi [sashes]); **Minamo** 27.

If you are here at the end of the day, especially on the weekend, this area will be humming with life in a way that is about as chilled as Tokyo gets. Relax and enjoy. ⬢

MEGURO
& EBISU

 **Ebisu Station** 29

13
14
15

25
24

12

11
10
17
9
8
18
16
7
20
6
21
19
22
23

Meguro Station

KEY

1	Claska Hotel	17	Chambre de nîmes brocante
2	Do	18	Junks
3	Fusion Interiors	19	Gallery. S
4	Otsu furniture	20	Brunch + time
5	Geographica	21	brunch + works
6	Catii Tokyo	22	Point no. 39
7	Pour Annick	23	Antoine Careme
8	Blackboard by karf	24	Boulangerie Jolly
9	Brunch + one	25	Kunima Coffee
10	Fake Furniture	26	Aburamen Park
11	Moody's	27	Neiro
12	Sonechika	28	Gakugeidaigaku Station
13	Silk	29	Ebisu Station
14	Lewis	30	Hara Museum of Contemporary Art
15	karf		
16	Brunch + sc		

30

In recent times, **Meguro** has earned itself a reputation as a hub for antique furniture and vintage goods—both local and international finds. Meguro Dori runs through the centre of town, perpendicular to the river. A wide boulevard, it's lined on both sides, for over a kilometre, with stores of well-priced, sought-after, old and new interior decorating items.

Meguro is not necessarily the first place people consider when planning a visit to Tokyo. But if you wish to be a little distanced from the throng during your stay, it is a worthy base. Not to mention home to the cool, almost cultish Claska Hotel. Accommodation aside, it boasts one of the best Japan-made 'souvenir' shops in town.

In the backstreets of Meguro, just north of Meguro Dori, lies a sleepy village promising a little magic and great coffee, to reward more relaxed and curious travellers.

The Meguro River, which links to small but groovy Naka Meguro (p92), is lined with breath-taking cherry blossoms in the springtime, making its riverbanks a favourite place for locals to stroll.

Neighbouring **Ebisu** is home to Yebisu beer, a few decent galleries and shopping options, but during the day it's more of a business hub. After dark is when Ebisu comes to life, with cheap and friendly food offerings and a plentiful, eclectic bar scene without the attitude, well, with one or two exceptions—but that can also provide an entertainment source of its own if you'll allow it …

SUGGESTED WALK

Depart via the west exit of **Meguro Station** ⊖ and jump in a cab for a quick ride along Meguro Dori to the **Claska Hotel** ❶. The sunny café/bar on the ground floor of the hotel is a pleasant spot to stop for a drink—day or night.

If you have an irresistible urge to immerse yourself in the craftiest creativity and Japanese design goods, go directly to gallery shop **Do** ❷ on the second floor. However, I warn you now that you will not be able to leave without purchasing something for yourself and anyone you consider a friend, which may weigh you down considerably. So if your core mission is to seek out antiquities and furniture, leave this shop until you are heading home.

Stay on the same side of the road as the hotel and take a quick detour right onto Meguro Dori towards **Fusion Interiors** ❸ then **Otsu furniture** ❹ a bit further along for both contemporary and vintage Japanese furniture. Then walk back in the direction of **Meguro Station** ❺.

On this side of the street, you'll find stores mainly focused on contemporary Japanese furniture and designer homewares—plus more 'everyday' lines (think a Japanese version of Ikea). In between are offerings ranging from period European furniture ❺ to Chinese ceramic vases ⓭. There's a fun/quirky décor and gift-centric shop, too ❿—oh, and just for good measure, a really neat denim store ❻ —not just well-made jeans but attractive denim shirts and soft shoes and accessories, such as satchels, too.

In between are offerings ranging from period European furniture to Chinese ceramic vases.

We all have different decorating tastes of course, but here are my personal picks along this route on the north side of Meguro Dori, in west-to-east order: **Geographica** ❺; **Catii Tokyo** ❻; **Pour Annick** ❼; **Blackboard by karf** ❽; **Brunch + one** ❾; **Fake Furniture** ❿; **Moody's** ⓫; **Sonechika** ⓬; **Silk** ⓭; **Lewis** ⓮; **karf** ⓯.

Just past **karf** ⓯, cross to the opposite side of Meguro Dori at the lights. Walk back towards the **Claska Hotel** ❶, past the Ootori Shrine and curious-sounding Parasite Museum (no, I've never brought myself to visit, although I hear it is interesting …). On this side of the street you'll find a smaller but even more eclectic group of shops focusing on furnishings and décor, with strong French and Scandinavian influences—both new and vintage; contemporary Japanese homewares and furniture (some made to order ⓳);

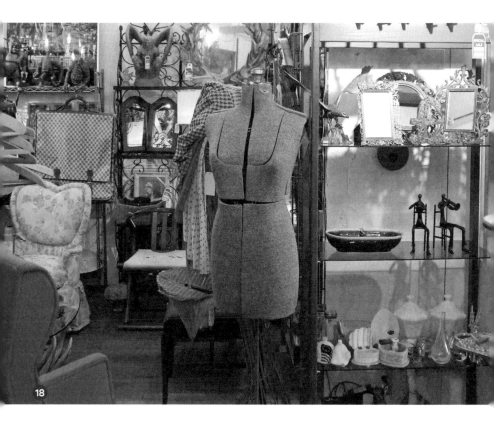

vintage bicycles **22**; and some highly collectible Americana so-called junk **18**—signs, lamps, toys etc. Here are my picks: **Brunch + sc 16**; **Chambre de nîmes brocante 17**; **Junks 18**; **Gallery. S 19**; **Brunch + time 20** and **brunch + works 21**; **Point no. 39 22**.

By this stage you may well be overcome with visions of yesteryear and in need of sweet sustenance. Duck into the side street west of **Point no. 39 22**. The cabinets at **Antoine Careme 23** are filled with marvellously delicious cakes, desserts, biscuits and oh-so-fine chocolates to take with you.

Back in front of **Point no. 39 22**, hop across Meguro Dori on a slight angle to your right and take the street under the green entrance posts with red and white signage. Walk 50 metres in this quaint backstreet to **Boulangerie Jolly 24** *(closed Tuesdays)*. Grab some plump savoury buns (oyatsu pan) and mini sandwiches at the old-fashioned bakery.

If you take the next street to your left after Boulangerie Jolly you'll discover a few quiet little cafés and restaurants. I love the tiny **Kunima Coffee ㉕**. The owner slowly, and ever so carefully, prepares your brew while you take in the peaceful room, despite the curious surgical-chic décor, and finger through some of his artsy library.

This neighbourhood is visually interesting for the funky 1950s- to 1970s-style architecture and the small country-town-like businesses run by local obaachan (grandmothers). The lovely green **Aburamen Park ㉖** is waiting for you to enjoy some R&R with your picnic stash. Afterwards, walk through the park, turn left at the carpark, and then continue for about 500 metres in a southwesterly direction until you reach an elegant bamboo garden on your right—part of the Central Ryokuchi Park. Opposite is perky vintage clothing store **Neiro ㉗**. A few steps further west are more cafés, should you need another cuppa.

If at this point you've already swallowed a whole day buying suitcase stuffers, you might choose to head towards **Gakugeidaigaku Station** ㉘, which is just a short distance from here. Follow a map app to find your way, as there are too many strangely angled streets to throw off your inner compass—but the meander through hushed back streets is a lovely foil to the busy main road. There are plenty of dining options around the station area if you'd like to stop before heading home with your goodies, at least the ones you haven't shipped back in a container. You'll get to experience a real 'salaryman' shuffle around dinnertime as workers head home from the station.

Perhaps you've gone light on the shopping and plan to hop directly over to Ebisu to kick your evening off with a refreshing tipple. If that's the case, grab a bus or taxi from the main road back to **Meguro Station** 🚇 and take the Yamanote train line just one stop (2–3 minutes) to **Ebisu Station** ㉙.

I f you had your fill of retro dreaming earlier in the day, check the exhibition schedule for the **Hara Museum of Contemporary Art** ㉚ in nearby Shinagawa before your Ebisu visit. It is situated in a Bauhaus-inspired building constructed as a private residence in the Showa period (1926–89). The nooks and crannies of the building itself are fabulous to explore, but its eclectic collection from local and international artists, such as Jackson Pollock, Anish Kapoor and Andy Warhol, is impressive. Hara regularly hosts exhibitions of new, cutting-edge talent. Some of its more confronting showings both enthral and slightly annoy me, but that's the beauty of art and expression and the emotions it can elicit. The café is a sweet spot to take tea and an exhibition-themed dessert. The museum shop is teensy, but top-notch for both exhibition paraphernalia and design gift items. ●

Ebisu

Tokyo Metro Hibiya Line

🚃 **Ebisu Station**

Yamanote Line

KEY

1 Yebisu Garden Place
2 Mitsukoshi
  Department Store
3 Tokyo Metropolitan
  Museum of
  Photography
4 Museum of
  Yebisu Beer
5 Cavo
6 Pile Café
7 Ebisu Yokocho
8 Bar Martha

1

SUGGESTED WALK

When you arrive at **Ebisu Station** 🚇, look for the signs that direct you through the recently refurbished and glamorous Artre shopping centre towards **Yebisu Garden Place** ❶, south of the station. Here you'll find an arced collection of buildings of varying purpose, from offices and shops to galleries and restaurants, all connected by a large open-air forecourt. It is quite a walk, so they've conveniently provided Yebisu Skyroad, a covered moving walkway, for which you will likely be grateful at this stage in proceedings.

There are several uninspiring shops around the Garden Place, but if food is your thing, check out the Depachika (basement food hall) in the **Mitsukoshi Department Store** ❷ for beautifully packaged

YEBISU

Japanese ingredients and pre-prepared foods. Many Japanese department stores have the most incredible food halls you can imagine, so make sure you wander around at least one during your stay.

For the highly visual with an interest in both contemporary and historic archival photography, I recommend the **Tokyo Metropolitan Museum of Photography ❸**.

Many Japanese department stores have the most incredible food halls you can imagine ...

The town of Ebisu (also known as Yebisu) was actually named after the beer company Yebisu, whose emblem is Ebisu, one of the seven Japanese gods of fortune. The original brewery kicked off the infrastructure in this part of Tokyo towards the end of the 1800s, when the station was built to service the rapidly expanding business. As homes and industry started to spring up around the station, the area itself also took on the name Ebisu. The handsome and well-organised **Museum of Yebisu Beer ❹**, which stands in **Garden Place ❶**, is surprisingly interesting—even for a non-beer drinker. If you are a connoisseur, you'll want to wet your whistle at the tasting area. Tickets can be purchased from vending machines. The tour looks like a lot of fun but at the time of printing is only offered in Japanese. There is good historical information and labelling of memorabilia available in English as you wander around. And a neat little gift store with stylish drinking paraphernalia. It's a fun aperitif to an Ebisu evening.

When you're ready to move on into the night, return to **Ebisu Station ⓔ** and head down the escalators to the west exit. On the right you'll find the fulsome Ebisu statue, which is a popular meeting point. Just past the statue, cross the road at Komazawa Dori and explore the back streets north of the main road—lined with many little bars and restaurants.

For a glass of wine and a nibble à la française try **Cavo ❺**. Across the road is **Pile Café ❻** for well-priced cocktails in a lofty (for Tokyo) space decorated in typical Japanified retro style, full of old couches and nanna lamps.

Return to Komazawa Dori and walk under the tunnel beneath the railway tracks. Take the second street on your right. On your left, before the 7-Eleven, is an entrance to **Ebisu Yokocho ❼**—a covered alleyway with about twenty tiny izakaya-type restaurant/bars. Izakaya traditionally refers to a place for sake, which serves food to go with it, but these days it is a more generic term for where you go to eat small dishes of food while drinking the beverage of your choice. Usually, this is sake, beer or chuuhai (shochu plus a flavoured spirit, syrup or juice, such as fresh grapefruit or orange, topped with soda water). There are more modern, stylised versions and chains, but this rustic type of izakaya enclave is curiously seductive in its raw and boisterous beauty. It's the perfect way to mingle with the locals up close over a few sticks of grilled pork or beef tongue, oden (a hotpot of seafood or meat, vegetables and tofu simmered in dashi), small dressed vegetable and pickle dishes, sushi or other quick bites. Bar hopping is perfectly acceptable to make a meal of it. You might find yourself eating some foods you've never tried before, so if you are squeamish about horsemeat or offal, I'd take a friend who speaks Japanese to avoid an ordering faux pas.

This rustic type of izakaya enclave is curiously seductive in its raw and boisterous beauty.

After dinner, for something completely different, leave the way you came in, turn left and head down the road for about 250 metres, until you hit a large intersection. There'll be a big Mizuhu Bank branch on the left corner. Walk around it, hugging it closely on your left and keep walking into the street that runs beside it. In about 70 metres **Bar Martha ❽** will be on your right. Look for the understated BAR sign.

Bar Martha is one seriously cool drinking hole. It's connected to the Martha records label, so the music selection is superb—the kind of mix you'd be happy to listen to all night, heavy on the jazz. The walls are lined with a vinyl library of which any music nerd would be jealous, and the drinks are primo quality. I highly recommend the 'rock'-style mojitos—on a large rock of ice without additional mixer—or the spicy Ginger Moscow Mule—they steep loads of fresh ginger in the alcohol in oversized jars you'll see around the place.

8

Canisters adorn every table for self-service nuts, rice crackers and chocolate, and the vibe is dark and sexy. However, go for the music, not to chat. Nicely marrying into the Zen Buddhist philosophy that you need to experience challenge and difficulty to appreciate the good in life, there is a downside to the Bar Martha experience—should you choose to see it that way. You MUST be on your best behaviour: to laugh or talk louder than the record is sacrilegious, and you will quickly be obviously and embarrassingly shooshed in the hope you will leave. If you attempt to take a photo you will be shot a piercing glare that clearly says—do it and die. It's not a bar for warm, friendly service or gaiety as such, but boy, it is damn fine for everything else. A most excellent way to end a long day. Just keep it down, will you? ●

KICHIJOJI, KOENJI & NAKANO

Kichijoji

Kichijoji Station

Kichijoji Dori

Heiwa Dori (Nakamichi)

Inokashira Dori

Chuo Main Line

Kichijoji Dori

Inokashira Park

KOENJI & NAKANO →

N

If I were forced to choose just one Tokyo suburb as a weekend base for a little R&R, it would probably be **Kichijoji**. This is the place to wander in and out of top-notch shops that range from elegant to funky, indulge in some fun eating and drinking, and engage in a bit of local village-hopping. It's only 15–20 minutes by train west of Shinjuku, or northwest of Shibuya, yet it feels so very far from the electric city.

This vibrant town, dotted with attractive commissioned graffiti art, was one of my favourite spots in my early twenties, and over twenty years later Kichijoji still grabs me. It's grown up with me in a way. What was a slightly grungy, alternative and quiet suburb has evolved into a sophisticated town with an infectiously sunny disposition, a chilled-out vibe and edge of curiosity. It has all the elements for a good time-out, including sprawling, leafy Inokashira Park.

Four stops east, back towards Shinjuku, you'll spot where the grunge cloud that once hung over **Kichijoji** has floated. Koenji is where the cool kids dabble in subculture and shop for thrifty pre-loved threads, quirky paraphernalia and vintage records.

Koenji is *the* place to find an incredible array of pastel to psychedelic shades of yesteryear, from 1950s glam and Rockabilly slick to 1970s swagger and 1980s New Romantics—with shoes, hats, footwear and belt buckles to match. There's enough of a thwack of Americana toys and cultural memorabilia to temp hobbyists or serious collectors too.

The cutting-edge Tokyo youth-with-attitude and their entrancing energy—a combination of 'Don't look at me … No, look at me!' and 'I'm embarrassing my parents and I don't give an expletive, please-thank-you'—have been transported here from the Harajuku (p28) of old. In the evenings there is a respectable jazz scene. Copious small bars and live houses are tucked into alleyways on the north side of the station, in which you can tap your tootsies alongside the local bohemians—if you're not low-grade headbanging to Japanese-style punk.

Back towards the city is **Nakano,** just one stop from Shinjuku and one of Tokyo's most populated suburbs. Nakano is the home of one seriously gigantic 'otaku' (in polite terms a nerd/enthusiast bordering on obsession) haven, spilling over with old and new figurines, manga, anime and slightly creepy dolls.

What's not to love about this gloriously eclectic suburb hop? There's certainly something for everyone in Tokyo's wild northwest, including relatively few tourists—for the moment …

SUGGESTED WALK

For me, the perfect day in Kichijoji starts with a stroll in the park before the shops open. Grab a coffee and a pastry from the **Rose Bakery ❶** in the delectable food hall underneath **Kichijoji Station ◷**—part of the stylish **Artre shopping mall ❷.** The mall is lined with a huge selection of tempting shops, from fashions to homewares, and casual, buzzing cafés and restaurants. Take the south (or the park) exit.

Cross the street and head down the laneway; you'll see a building with the letters OIOI directly ahead—this is the **Marui department store ❸.** You are now on Inokashira Dori. Cross over and take the walkway that runs along the right-hand side of **Marui ❸.** After a few minutes you'll walk past some shops and cafés.

7

Take note of **L'epicurien** ❹ on the right, as you may wish to return here after the park—it's a long-standing favourite patisserie and café of mine, but some days it's a little slow to open. Snaffle some of their divine chocolates too, for later on.

In no time at all you'll be at the top of the stairs that lead to **Inokashira Park** ❺. If it's spring, you'll be greeted by the first of many blossom trees as you enter the green space. Find a bench by the pond and take in the view. If you have time, walk the whole way around the pond, or at least check out the greener part in the centre, perhaps strolling as far as the colourful **Inokashira Benzaiten** ❻ temple and back again. If you are in the Benzaiten vicinity, and the **Ghibli Museum** ❼ is on your agenda, you'll see signposts for it everywhere in the park. I don't wish to dash anybody's dreams regarding the cartoon-like building's ode to the animations and art of the beloved and uber-talented Hayao Miyazaki, but—if I may be

so bold—you'll probably enjoy this experience best if you meet the sub-1-metre height requirement for climbing on the giant plush toy Catbus. Booking ahead is essential.

The park is beautiful in bloom, when it is also most busy. It is also particularly green and cooling in the summer months, and utterly peaceful in the colder months—rug up and have the place to yourself.

When the time is right, head back up the steps past a jumble of cafés, boho-style shops and pop-up stores, back to the main road. Cut through the station and out via the north exit—that's if you don't find yourself lingering around the glamorous station precinct, home to **Artre shopping mall ❷**.

Just left of the north exit is **Nippon Department Store ❽** (also at Aki-Oka designer precinct p231, but here you'll find a more varied product range). They sell excellent traditional and contemporary Japanese handicrafts, homewares and a few regional ingredients.

Step out of the shop and straight ahead is a bus terminal. Directly to the left of it, you can't miss the sign for the **Sun Road Shotengai ❾** entrance—a rather daggy old shopping arcade that is due for a facelift any day, but provides a good idea of typical everyday Tokyo suburban life.

Cross the road (Heiwa Dori) but instead of going into the Sun Road Shotengai take the first left. Within a couple of shops you'll spot **Tansu-ya ❿** on your left, specialising in second-hand kimono— definitely worth a look. They aren't as cheap as others you can find, but they are very good quality and many look brand new.

Keep walking past the food vendors selling Japanese sweets, tea and the like. If you stumble across **Satou butcher's shop ⓫**, you may be curious to find a queue a mile long—apparently their minchi katsu (wagyu mince and potato cutlets—a type of croquette) are well worth the wait.

Turn left at Kichioji Dori, walking as far as the **PARCO department store** ⑫. Cross the street and **Uniqlo** ⑬ is on the corner. The window displays are always worth checking out, as are their casual basics—ever at bargain prices. Continue past Uniqlo into Nakamichi (middle street)—the old shotengai area of Heiwa Dori—on its left-hand side.

This is where things start to get a little more interesting in the shopping stakes. Mingling with the old family-run vegetable shops and gyoza shacks are stores packed with desirable goods and fashions.

To be clear, there are several fashion labels catering to a couple of quite specific audiences, namely fragile waifs who can make the white-lace-doily look sing, or beret-wearing new Japanese mums in denim dungarees, baggy mohair cardigans and le canvas sacs filled with boulangerie and baby wipes. I haven't focused on them myself—but don't let me stop you … If you are size S and into quality pretty or no-nonsense apparel, you'll be set.

There are too many shops in this area, including all the big name stores, to provide a thorough overview. The selection below will give you a base route to follow and venture from as the whim takes you.

About 100 metres along on your right is **L.Musee** ⓮, a store as small and cute as the new and vintage buttons it sells. There's a little ribbon and lace too.

Further down, past the post office you'll come to **Puku Puku** ⓯, a reasonably priced antique place selling mainly ceramics and laquerware. I'm prone to spending some time in this squeezy store packed with hand-painted plates, sake vessels, exquisitely well-preserved lacquered bowls and the odd wooden tray. Watch your elbows or you'll be paying for more than you bargained for!

Wickie ⓰ is on the left a little further along. It has a section of Scandilicious decorative and utilitarian goods that truly complement Japanese interiors and lifestyle.

A few stores down on the same side is **Pool2** ⑰—a gallery store that reaches new and artistic heights each month when it changes the well-compiled lifestyle collection by both local and foreign creators. The mother store and exhibition space Pool is further down the road.

Also on your left (just before the kids' park) is the relatively new **Margaret Howell** ⑱ shop and MHL café. The British designer is inspired by authenticity and nature, so her tastes are very much in sympatico with those of the Japanese—no doubt the reason her timeless clothing and accessories have been sold in Japan since the early 1980s. She now has ninety stores countrywide. There's also a handful of stylish modern Japanese cookware and tableware based on traditional pieces. If nostalgia has you hankering for a slice of quiche or scones with jam and cream, this might be an appropriate pit stop.

Walk almost to the end of Nakamichi shopping street, you'll see the name on its entrance archway. About-face and take a left at the colourful Cotswolds store—just for a quick look at the cute **Tsubame markt ⑲**. Although it sells mainly European antique knick-knacks and stationery, the styling of the store is a perfect example of the inherently clever Japanese way with small spaces.

Hop back onto Nakamichi and walk back the way you came. You'll see **Hara Doughnuts ⑳** on your left—sure, there are donuts all over the world, but these use all-natural ingredients with flavours such as green tea, black sugar, sesame, kinako (roasted soy bean flour) and even spinach or carrot!

Just past the **Margaret Howell ⑱** shop, turn right, and in a few steps you'll find a small arts and craft centre to your left. The first shop on your right as you step inside is **Bondo ㉑**—a handmade art store. There's not a lot of stock, but what they do have has been selected by someone with an eye for picking up clever and handsome goods from around Japan—mostly ceramics, jewellery and accessories.

Return to the main drag by taking a right. If it is possible for you to walk past **Kichijoji Tsuru's Original Roast Beans ㉒** without stopping to inhale, you are made of stronger stuff than I. A takeaway coffee would work perfectly with that donut you might have purchased earlier …

Continue past the post office just one short block, then quickly duck left. **Markus ㉓** is a small gallery-like store of modern, earthy ceramics, pretty hand-blown glass, artistic totes and other beautiful, functional items, such as traditional hand-woven brooms.

Return to Nakamichi, then take the next street left and follow it about 200 metres until you get to the Nike store, then take the next street on your left. In about 100 metres on your right you'll be in a little slice of kitchen to tableware heaven at **Cinq ㉔**—detectable only by the number 5 on the door. This stylish shop space is arranged beautifully with retro-inspired and modern cookware and homewares.

When you leave the store, go back the way you came, passing the corner where you turned near the Nike store, then take the next street on your left. In about 150 metres you will arrive at the

exceptional **OUTBOUND** ㉕. It might feel as though you're going to end up slap bang in the middle of suburbia as you wander towards the end of the street, but trust me—you'll want to know about this place. From made-to-order handcrafted shoes, which will likely outlast you and cost your life's savings, but are so beautiful you will just want to fondle them for hours, to smooth wooden bowls that vibrate with the essence of the trees from which they came, to exotic perfume inspired by Japanese cities, to lovingly woven bamboo baskets. Then there are the incredibly luxe linen shirts in shades of indigo, stone and wood, organic-looking ceramics and hand-painted gift cards. It is just a joy to be around this much creative dedication.

Turn left when you leave the store and left again onto the next street. When you get to the busy main road (Kichijoji Dori) take a right. On your left is a Buddhist temple complex. Paradoxically, there's an embarrassing amount of high-end international brand shopping just to the east of this area. Keep walking about 250 metres and you'll find yourself back at **PARCO** ⑫. Take a left here, heading back in the direction of **Kichijoji Station's** Ⓝ north exit.

modern, earthy ceramics, pretty hand-blown glass, artistic totes and other beautiful, functional items …

If you're wondering where the day has gone and the lights are starting to fade, you may feel the time is right for a beverage and a snackette. Conveniently, en route to the station on your left is **Harmonica Yokocho** ㉖, a small, warren-like precinct lined with tiny, rustic and some newer, flashier izakaya and bars. Although dead as a post during the day, by twilight its lanterns are popping to a glow and the grills are a-firing, ready for the onslaught of yakitori orders.

Go right ahead and wander through what is quite an exotic and mysterious atmosphere. Fortune tellers prepare for the evening, knowing old men perch themselves in prime position for acquiring the barkeep's attention, dumpling folders giggle over local gossip, and the pickle maker tends his wares with one eye glued to black-and-white re-runs on an ashtray-sized TV.

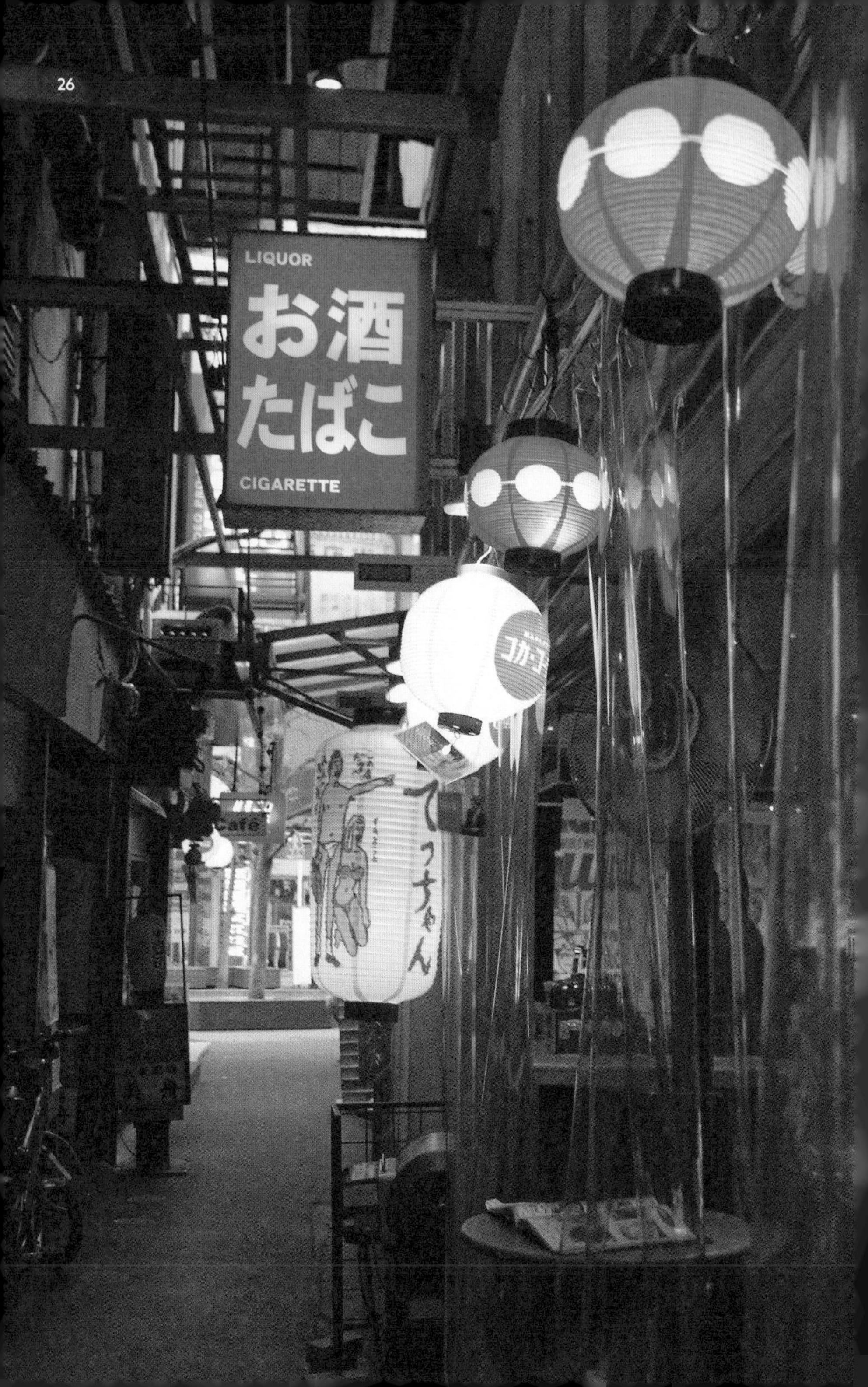
LIQUOR
お酒
たばこ
CIGARETTE
Café
てつちゃん

If the authenticity of night-time shanty life feels a bit daunting, you'll find more modern, light and breezy offerings closer to the station. While I might now boldly strut myself down alleys unknown, excited by the prospect of chatting with the regulars and finding something exotic to eat or drink (speaking the language certainly aids that), there were many years when I was intimidated to venture into such seemingly private, locals-only hidey-holes. So there will be no finger-wagging if you opt for the latter!

Kichijoji Station 🚇 is just ahead on your right. Feel free to jump ship whenever you are ready. ⬤

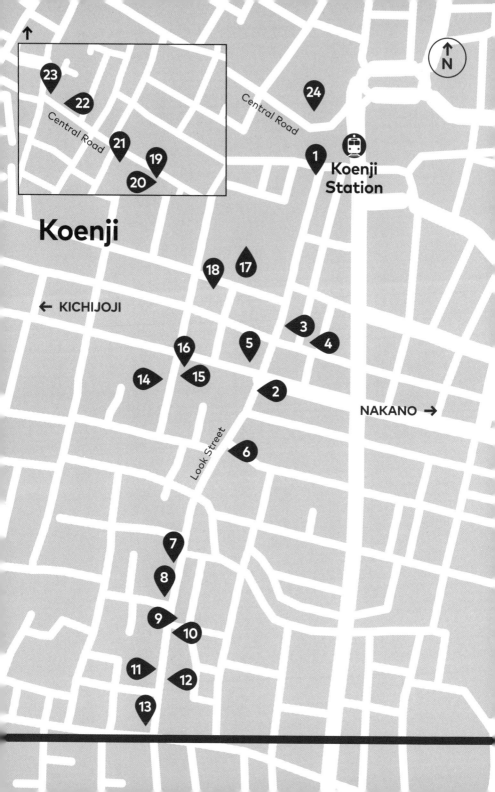

Koenji

Central Road

Central Road

Koenji Station

← KICHIJOJI

NAKANO →

Look Street

I f you've just stopped in to Kichijoji for a quick peek but are more interested in vintage attire and the edgier town of Koenji, hop on the train and travel four stops east on the JR Chuo line. Be aware that many of the vintage shops don't open until at least lunchtime.

SUGGESTED WALK

L eave the south exit of **Koenji Station** 🔵 and turn right. You'll see a set of traffic lights ahead, and just beyond it the entrance to the rather uninspiring **PAL shopping arcade** ❶ to your left. It is worth a glance left and right as you walk through—there is the occasional joy-spot to buy a cool T-shirt or some outrageously silly novelty items. However, it's the street that continues after the arcade stops, and the slightly bedraggled side alleys slinking off the main route, where the more intriguing sights and sounds of a bygone era reveal themselves to unsuspecting visitors.

Once the short PAL shopping arcade ends, a completely different, open-air shopping experience begins and runs for around 700 metres. Welcome to **Look Street** ❷. There's a party of shops here and dotted around the surrounding area, predominantly vintage or thrift-focused, with individual personalities from the soft and feminine to the freakster funky. No doubt you'll discover your own favourites; I've provided an eclectic cross-section to explore as you walk along.

It's a starter list—to try and cover everything here would be insane—besides, I need to let you uncover some treasures of your own! So get ready to bunny-hop, but do make sure to look up and

KEY

1   PAL shopping arcade
2   Look Street
3   Spank
4   Peep Cheep
5   The Village Vanguard
6   Zool
7   Lover Soul
8   Aileen
9   Adoluvle retrist
10 Kiki
11 Comyu handmade & Vintage
12 Kiarry's
13 Grandprix
14 Ehon Yarusuban
15 Gallery3 café
16 Mad Tea Party
17 Chosenji Temple
18 Used Clothing Suburbia
19 Hayatochiri
20 Southpaw
21 Nekono
22 Mikansei
23 Owl Café Baron
24 Sub Rosa

take in the bigger picture—the retro feel is enhanced by the gorgeous early 1900s architecture, which fortunately managed to avoid the Second World War bombings.

Let's step back and begin in the **PAL shopping arcade ❶**.

Spank ❸ promises the pretty pastel Lolita or baby-doll look. Note that it's worth ducking left into the street that runs just past this store to check out **Peep Cheep ❹**—for florals, paisley and plaid, plus complementary vintage jewellery. If you keep heading along that street and those that run off it, there's even more eye candy if you still have the energy after an already jam-packed day!

Back on course … **The Village Vanguard ❺** is always full of surprises, from the functional to the outrageous—music, books and manga to rock-star sunglasses and bright accessories.

And onto **Look Street ❷**: **Zool ❻**—vintage clothes and antique knick-knacks; **Lover Soul ❼**—groovy lady-frocks with all the hits

of the 1960s, 1970s and 1980s; **Aileen** ❽ (by grog grog)—antiques, bric-a-brac and American vintage apparel; **Adoluvle retrist** ❾—new clothes, think elegant smart casual coordinates; **Kiki** ❿—kawaii (cute) and colourful; **Comyu handmade & Vintage** ⓫—handmade and vintage frills, lace and fur; **Kiarry's** ⓬—vintage and collectable toys, signs, tableware; **Grandprix** ⓭—Brady Bunch eat your heart out.

When you reach the main street (Ome Highway), it's time to turn back. Walk as far as the takoyaki (octopus ball snack) stand—look for the red octopus on a yellow awning on your left-hand side on the corner of a cross street. Take the next street on your left. If you've gone as far as **The Village Vanguard** ❺ you've missed the turn-off by one block.

Walk past the post office, then take the next right—you are now in a seemingly run-down area. Look more closely, as there are some really nifty cafés, galleries and stores popping up. On your left you'll

see some dilapidated red stairs. Carefully climb them to the top, pretending you are in a tree house, and you'll enter a most endearing, whimsical picture-book shop—**Ehon Yarusuban** ⓮. There are vintage and new books with a strong focus on illustrated children's titles, and a small selection of gorgeous stationery too. A shy but sweet young fellow quietly mans the cash register, typical of the energy in this back pocket of Koenji, such a far cry from its neighbouring arcade, bristling with neon crimes and commercial branding.

A mere step across the laneway is **Gallery3 café** ⓯, the perfect spot to rest and refuel with excellent coffee. The proprietor speaks some English, and it's clear he has a local following of artists, some of whom exhibit in his teensy gallery. It really is such a tranquil pit stop. Watching your host slowly and exquisitely prepare your brew will instantly put you into a trance-like state of deepest relaxation.

Next door is **Mad Tea Party** ⓰ for a vintage and handmade collection of clothes and accessories inspired by Lewis Carroll's *Alice's Adventures in Wonderland*.

Carefully climb to the top, pretending you are in a tree house, and you'll enter a most endearing, whimsical picture book shop ...

Turn right at the next street, and then take the next left at the supermarket. Walk about a minute to **Chosenji Temple** ⓱ —the perfect spot for a shopping reprieve and to help deflect any guilt about cultural neglect. The afternoon light is particularly comforting and helps highlight some of the details you can miss at other times.

When you depart the temple, look right, in case there's some 1950s glamour on display at **Used Clothing Suburbia** ⓲. Regain your composure and head away from the temple gate towards the supermarket you passed earlier. Turning right at the shopping strip takes you back past more vintage and local food shops. Beyond that is a relaxed and friendly residential area, so take some time to explore here if you like.

Turning left at the shopping strip you came to outside **Chosenji Temple** ⓱ takes you back to the **PAL shopping arcade** ❶—via shops spilling over with second-hand sneakers and the like.

Walk in the direction of the train line and continue north through the underpass, taking a sharp left at the first street onto Central Road—you'll see an archway with a sign if you look up! You are now on a street that runs northwest. At first you'll see a lot of cheap and cheerful eateries and bars, followed swiftly by a multitude of barbers and hair salons. If you keep going you're in for a treat of even quirkier vintage stockists and curio stores. I'll leave you alone for a goggle-eyed wander this time.

However, do look out for the mixed bag of gobstopper vintage at **Hayatochiri** ⑲ in the chaotic Kitakore Building. You'll have little chance of missing it—just look for the monster green facade with giant eyes staring down at you, or the giant pink ice-cream cone of delight—it's about halfway along Central Road on your left. The building also houses **Southpaw** ⑳ (by Nincompoop Capacities) for offbeat new and vintage styles.

This next haunt should really not feature in a style guide, but it's so bad it's good. A few buildings along you'll see **Nekono** ㉑—a shop and gallery foaming at the mouth with cat-themed zakka (miscellaneous décor items) and handmade cat-worship art. This is so Tokyo, in an in-joke way, so in the spirit of curious Koenji, I simply had to include it.

Mikansei ㉒ and its random multicultural retro glam contribution to the strip is about the last stop on the retro/vintage/quirko express before you should make an about-face. Use the Sunkus convenience store at the T-intersection as your turning circle because it's probably beverage o'clock right about now and directly across the road, on the third floor, is **Owl Café Baron** ㉓.

However, if you don't fancy taking tea with an owl, start retracing your steps to the **Koenji Station** Ⓔ area—taking a peek into all the little lantern-lit alleyways. You'll encounter postage-stamp-sized bars and cafés, such as the très cute **Sub Rosa** ㉔ close to the station. Sit up at the counter sipping sake or refreshing red shiso juice over a few plates of creative Japanese snacks made from seasonal ingredients.

Once night has well and truly hit, sample the live music scene too. There are a couple of famous live houses, but keep your eyes and ears peeled for tucked-away, more intimate, laid-back venues.

Still hungry? As you make your way back to the station, slip down the alleyway to your right just before you exit Central Road (back

19

19

21

22

near where you first stepped onto it). You'll find yourself in a dingy under-track alleyway—gado-shita, literally, 'beneath the girders', lined with both seedy-looking and swanky small bars and places to eat. This section of the 'Koenji Street' dining precinct is a bit of the real and gritty Japan that tourists rarely see. (You'll find one of the more famous gado-shita examples under Yurakucho Station, not far from Tokyo Station.) It's a lot of fun to pull up a stool at the counter and slurp a bowl of ramen or order a few sticks of grilled wagyu and a cold beer. Abstaining is fruitless—the tempting aromas of sizzling garlicky meats and sweet soy-glazed yakitori will drive you insane. However, if that doesn't take your fancy there are a variety of restaurants and bars lining the south side of the tracks. When you are ready to move on, simply follow the signs to the station platform. ●

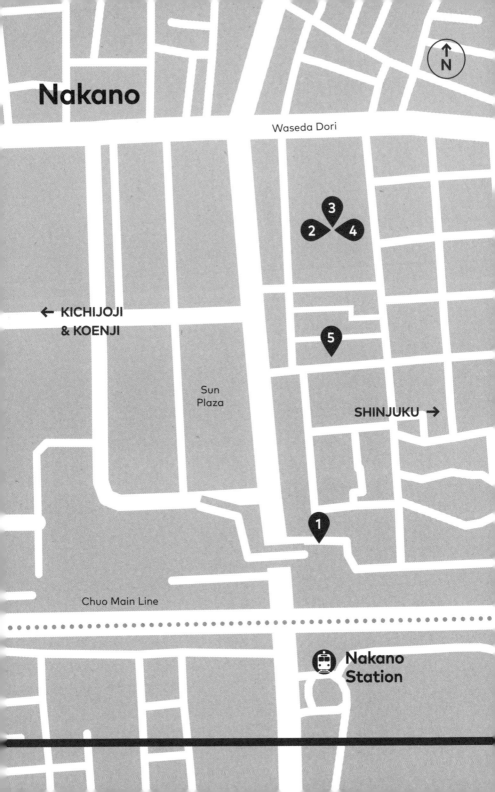

If your closet nerd (or travelling companion) feels compelled to take just one last stop, then jump back on the train one station to Nakano.

SUGGESTED WALK

Take the north exit of **Nakano Station** 🚇 and almost directly ahead, on the other side of the bus terminus, you'll see the arch of **Sun Mall** ❶—just to the right of the enormous Sun Plaza complex. Yes, there's a recurring theme in this part of Tokyo. Sun Mall, Sun Plaza, Sun Road, Sundays …

Enter the 'tastefully decorated' arcade and continue north all the way along it until you reach **Nakano Broadway** ❷—utopia to the doll curious; sorry, not dolls, collectables. Go crazy—there is floor after floor of items you can't really fathom ever needing in your life, yet certain folk (predominately menfolk) take them very seriously. Around the globe these old, and sometimes new, figures, toys, games and oddities are traded for hard cash as they increase in value—in many cases this occurs over more years than you may survive. Or these items sit on shelves, collecting more dust than funds, in their pristine packaging until someone (sensibly) tidies them into a bin. You may sense a touch of first-hand experience regarding a certain style of man-cave beautification. Each to their own—we all have our vices.

On a far more serious and fair note, the place is spectacular on an experiential level. You will not have imagined anything like it. I'll even admit to appreciating Japanese vintage tin toys, old Tokyo street signs and even some creepy dolls. Photo opportunities!

KEY

1 Sun Mall
2 Nakano Broadway
3 Back to MONO
4 MMTS
5 Teketeke Izakaya

Nakano Broadway also boasts some interesting hobby and gift stores. My favourites are **Back to MONO ❸**, featuring items that might well be at home in a modern art gallery, and **MMTS ❹**—just because … you'll see.

There are also several vinyl outlets for those who dig their music old-school. And if you are old enough to remember classic arcade games, such as the mega-addictive Space Invaders, Pac-Man and Frogger, you can revisit your childhood for a moment and flick that joystick till the cows come home.

On your way back to **Nakano Station ☺** and in need of some soul-cleansing fried chicken or hard liquor? Exit **Nakano Broadway ❷** at the point you entered—re-entering **Sun Mall ❶**. Take the fourth alleyway on your left and you'll soon locate **Teketeke Izakaya ❺**. Specialising in grilled and fried tori (chicken), it's guaranteed to satisfy. ●

KAGURAZAKA & KORAKUEN

T his place holds a charm that is often difficult to locate in the bright and shiny capital. The zigzagging, delightfully ad-hoc stone pathways, hidden nooks and quiet but attractive residential laneways provide an atmosphere closer to the more traditional, low-rise city of Kyoto.

The hillside perch of **Kagurazaka** is home to a mere handful of geisha houses and ryotei—traditional restaurants featuring exquisite Kaiseki cuisine— compared to what stood here long ago. During the Edo period (1603–1867) an elegant and thriving quarter existed for the entertainment of the samurai, who resided on the outskirts of Edo Castle—home to the Shogun at the time. Much of the castle has been destroyed but some sections still stand in the grounds of the nearby Imperial Palace.

While there is an increasing number of modern shopping opportunities and cafés in Kagurazaka, there are plenty of traditional shops selling foods and everyday necessities. You'll spot more neatly kimono-wrapped older women with perfectly coiffed hair than anywhere else in Tokyo. I imagine it's a knock-on geisha effect.

In the evening, particularly on the weekends, the place takes on a different ambience and excitement. On weekdays, it is quiet compared with other Tokyo suburbs, and a place to wander in contemplation, weaving in and out of several of the temples and shrines in close proximity. Certain streets are closed off on weekends, making way for pedestrian traffic and a charming handicrafts market.

In the 1950s, the Institut Français was built in the area by the French government to help introduce its language and culture. It resulted in the development of a large expat community. French-accented hints dot the streets by way of restaurants, cafés, patisseries and fromageries. The romance of the area is furthered by Kagurazaka's link to a literary past due to the number of publishing houses established here—it is said that many writers and poets have been drawn to reside here. It's not difficult to understand why.

SUGGESTED WALK

By now you'll have likely assessed that I love to start or interrupt my busy Tokyo days by breathing in a bit of nature or immersing myself briefly in some form of culture. For me, a visit to the Kagurazaka area would not be complete without a stroll through the beautiful **Koishikawa Korakuen Garden** ❶, one of the oldest and best-preserved gardens in Tokyo. Designed with Confucian sensibilities, construction of the garden began in the 1600s but was not completed for decades, and only opened to the public in 1938.

To access the garden, leave **Iidabashi Station** ❹ via the C3 Exit— important, as it is a long walk if you leave through the wrong end of the station. Take a right, then first left and within 100 metres on your right will be the entrance to the garden.

Korakuen, as it is more commonly known, is one of the few places where you can feel distanced from the intensity of Tokyo, even though you are still very much in it. It is humbling just to be in one of Tokyo's few surviving Edo-period gardens. It's larger than it first appears, and although it may be tempting to simply walk around the central garden, the nooks and gardens in the outer pockets hold the most intrigue and beauty. Keep an eye out for the subtle wooden signposts. Bridges, ponds, blossom groves, pine trees, moss-cloaked rocks, gentle dancing leafy shadows, and space to breathe—somewhat of a luxury in Tokyo.

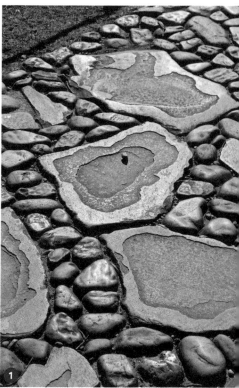

In winter the garden is stark and desirably quiet—a smattering of snow and a lake iced over in parts with tiny buds huddling in preparation for spring have a certain beauty one must witness to understand. If you are lucky, your walk will be accompanied by the faint sound of classical music from the Tokyo Dome right next door. From certain vantage points the skyscraper backdrop provides a surreal contrast and a reminder of what lies beyond the garden gates.

To save time and your feet, take a taxi south along Sotobori Dori's wide boulevard until you reach the furthest southwest point of **Iidabashi Station** ⊕. Standing with your back to busy West Exit (B2a), you'll see the popular **Canal Café** ❷ straight ahead—an excellent place to caffeinate yourself post walk. In warmer weather make the most of the outdoor seating by the water.

Directly across the main road, at the traffic lights, you'll see a rather spiffy, wood-panelled Starbucks on the corner of Sotobori

and Waseda Dori. Cross to here and walk up Waseda Dori. You are now gently heading up what is also referred to as Kagurazaka Naka Dori—translating as the middle street of the Kagura slope. Kagura is the name for ancient Shinto music—it is said it could once be heard emanating from Edo Castle by those on the zaka (slope).

Although half a day should give you a good sense of the area, if you have the time, this is the perfect part of Tokyo to get lost in, wandering wherever the laneways lead you. As long as you keep returning to the central slope you'll never veer too far off track. In this visually compelling neighbourhood you'll one minute be tottering in tiny cobbled laneways so trim your shoulders almost touch the walls, and the next you'll have turned a corner to face a large and stunning contemporary architectural structure. It is a fun and energising neighbourhood to explore.

The initial part of the slope and off-shoot laneways feel a little like your average Chinatown, with a number of cuisine-appropriate eateries and food stalls dotted between flower vendors and incense stores, supermarkets, patisseries, and traditional Japanese rice cracker and wagashi (confectionery) shops.

Not far up the slope on the left, wafting perfume will draw your attention to **Tsubaki-ya ❸**—a small shop on the ground floor of the Miyasaka building selling a wide selection of incense in handsome packaging. It offers an assortment of other living-space improvements, including some stunning, seasonally inspired washi (paper) products. The Japanese believe that scent brings a certain personality to your surrounds and enables you to express yourself non-verbally.

As you exit Tsubaki-ya you'll see a red wall-tiled building opposite, housing a shop famous for Chinese-style steamed buns. **GOJUUBAN honten ❹** (main shop) sells a selection of sweet and savoury fillings—from custard and sweet azuki beans to slow-cooked pork in soy, tiny dried fish and modern inclusions, such as mozzarella—popular with the younger crowd. Devour one while they are hot or grab a take-home pack.

It's rather like stepping back in time; squint to imagine a geisha shuffling through these laneways in twilight.

Take the immediate right to detour down the lantern-lined street of Honda Yokocho—named after a samurai who resided here. It hosts around fifty wall-to-wall eateries and bars, which come to life after sunset. Off to the right are two cobblestoned alleyways for exploring. Geisha Shinmichi is the first to your right, past the steamed bun place. Kakurenbo, or Embo yokocho (hide-and-seek alley), is a little further along on your right. It's rather like stepping back in time; squint to imagine a geisha shuffling through these laneways in twilight. Look out for **Makanai ❺**, natural Japanese cosmetics made from ingredients such as green tea, konnyaku starch and yuzu (Japanese citrus).

Continue up the main slope of Waseda Dori. Within moments you'll be in front of popular temple **Zenkoku-ji ❻**—home to Bishamon-sama, the protective deity of Kagurazaka, who has apparently been granting worshippers good luck for over 200 years. The large red gate at the front is known as Bishamonten. It's a common meeting place—if you're with a group, make this your reconnection spot if someone gets lost.

三十番 神楽坂本店
焼きそばまん
¥340 (税込) ¥315(本体価格)

三十番 神楽坂本店
モッツァレラチーズまん
¥290 (税込) ¥269(本体価格)

¥287(本体価格)

三十番 神楽坂本店
あんまん
¥370 (税込) ¥343(本体価格)

三十番 神楽坂本店
ピリ辛肉まん

4

5

COSMETICS

MAKANAI

まかないじ

3

伽羅
stick

沈香

沈香

一位香

10

7

9

(本体 3,030円)

明寺

ち

もち

いす

I f you skipped the buns in favour of something appropriately French and are starting to feel a little peckish, you are in the perfect place to access one of Kagurazaka's most popular crepe spots—**Le Bretagne** ❼. Cross the road from the temple to the Chinese restaurant (Torijaya Honten). Hop down the short alley that runs alongside the restaurant and in 20 metres you'll find some fine Breton-style buckwheat galettes with both savoury (think French jambon and cheese) and sweet fillings. These are available in affordable courses with sides, all washed down with a good cider. However, if you haven't booked, be there when it opens, as it packs out within minutes. The signature dessert crepe with salted butter caramel ice cream is delectable.

Return to **Zenkoku-ji** ❻ and take the alley that runs along side it. When you come to the first cross street turn right, and just a few shops down on your left is **La Ronde d'Argile** ❽. This is an excellent gallery space with stunningly crafted ceramic, wood, metalwork and glass serveware, and décor designed with traditional Japanese and French aesthetics in mind.

Return to the temple gate and continue up the hill. You'll soon come to **Isuzu** ❾ on your left, a famous old sweets shop. If you haven't tried traditional wagashi (Japanese confectionery) you really must—the faintly pink-tainted sakura mochi (cherry-blossom-flavoured rice and bean sweets, wrapped in aromatic cherry tree leaves) or sweet soy-glazed mitarashi dango would be superb with a cup of green tea back in your room.

Ahead on your right in about 250 metres is an even quainter wagashi shop, called **Baikatei** ❿. Its servers are almost as sweet as its wares. The seasonal displays are pretty as a picture. While the shop is over eighty years old—founded in 1935—its modern takes on tradition, such as perfectly executed thimble-sized strawberries made from white bean paste with freeze-dried strawberry pieces, are a delightful invention and make the perfect gift for a hostess.

A couple of shops later, on the opposite side of the road, you will see a great Japanese supermarket called **Kimuraya** ⓫. This place is not only handy for stocking your hotel bar fridge but as a marker for this winding walk. Do not even glance in the direction of the **Little Mermaid Bakery** ⓬ across the road if you are craving sweet pastries—you'll want to buy the store.

On the street just southwest of **Kimuraya** ⓫, there are a couple of shops worth noting. About 100 metres along you'll find a

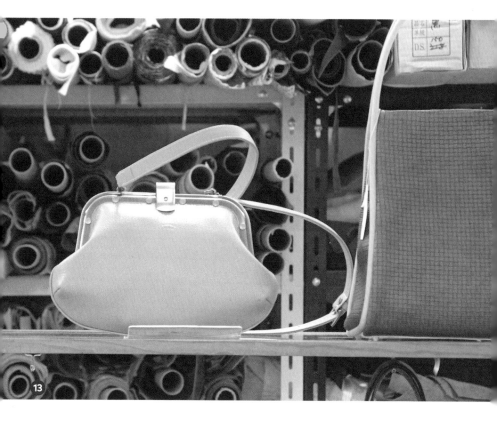

leather-craft business and shop called **Craftman Manou** ⓭. Look for the red awning and peek through the window, where you are likely to see the man himself tinkering away. The shop owner and his wife arc a friendly team selling their made-to-order leather and fabric bags. There are a few items on the shelves, including some cute purses he prepared earlier, to snap up straight away if you don't have time to wait!

On the same side of the street is the very sweet and very French-sounding **La Terre** ⓮. It features Japanese ceramics in contemporary styles—soba cups, sake flasks and handsome nabe (hotpot vessels)—with natural glazes and colours.

The temple across the road is **Enfukutera and enpukuji** ⓯. You'll know it by the stunning etchings on metal at the front gate depicting some history of the local area. Once you reach this, turn around and return to **Kimuraya** ⓫.

Continue a couple of blocks along and at the traffic lights turn right at the Sunkus convenience store. You will see a large red torii gate ahead of you. This is the entrance to the **Akagi Jinja** ⓰—Akagi Shinto shrine—most striking for its modernity, which somehow merges harmoniously into its urban backdrop. I've never seen another shrine quite like this in Japan—constructed of glass, honeyed wood and a modern steel roof. The shrine, reportedly seven centuries old, was redeveloped from its relatively run-down state in 2010 by famous contemporary architect Kengo Kuma (who also designed the Nezu Museum p71 and Asakusa Cultural Information Centre p198). It is considered the true heart and protector of Kagurazaka.

Adjacent is a block of apartments built to help fund the project. In its basement is the light and airy **Akagi café** ⓱—not a bad place to rest your feet and linger over your spiritual views and a glass of wine. What an extraordinary concept.

18 | 19

Once a month the shrine hosts a small handicrafts market. It's held on irregular days, from 10 am to 5 pm, so check the market's blog (using Google translate) for updates: **akagimarche.blogspot.jp/**

Return to the main drag again and take a right to continue up the hill. If good coffee is calling your name right about now, I highly recommend **Bon Riviere** ❶⑧—their iced coffee is sensational on a warm day, and their chocolates and cake are delicious too, but their teeny fruit-based meringues are out of this world. Get some in you.

About 100 metres up the road you'll come to a set of lights. On the right is an entrance to Kagurazaka Station—just near McDonald's—and on your left, up an attractive set of wide, wooden steps inspired by the Spanish Steps in Rome, is the intelligent and beautiful **Le Kagu** ❶⑨. It bears the nickname given to Kagurazaka by the French, who found the word a bit of a tongue-twister. Housed in a contemporary-looking warehouse space once belonging to a

publishing company and also designed by local architect Kengo Kuma (*see* Akagi Jinja p185)—much of the critically lauded original structure has been retained. The entire concept of the store is renewal and revalue—mixing old with the new around the topics of life's essentials—clothing, shelter, food and knowledge. The sharing of information is important to the owners. They hold regular author events on the second floor beside their micro bookstore of ten carefully selected titles by ten carefully selected authors—some famous, some just from the 'hood'. Genres span lifestyle, art and design, philosophy and Japanese culture.

The fashion and furnishing items come from European and Japanese designers. The homewares section hosts a covetable range of new and antique objects, selected by the store's fashion stylist. An inviting café serves hotdogs, fries and coffee—'because that's the reality of how young Japanese eat'—but all the sausages are

handcrafted using authentic European recipes. It's easy to spend a lot of time and substantial yen in this seriously handsome store.

By now you could be laden with shopping bags, so you may wish to hop straight onto a train—so simply go back down the stairs and directly into Kagurazaka Station. However, if you feel like strolling around the peaceful, often rustic residential area, why not casually explore the winding laneways south and east of **Le Kagu** ⑲?

If it is dinnertime, return to the front of **Kimuraya** ⑪ once again and take the street just below it, but this time heading northeast. Follow the road as it turns and a little way up the hill you will spot a black fence and the entrance to **KADO** ⑳. This casual, traditional Japanese restaurant inside an old house serves simple, fresh home cooking. Lunch set plates feature inexpensive items such as donburi (rice bowls topped with some form of protein) or omu rice (omelette wrapped around seasoned rice). Dinner set courses

featuring duck, quail, pork or seafood nabe (a simmered hotpot dish) are also very reasonable.

The atmosphere is worth the price alone—rarely do you find this kind of experience in Tokyo—it's tucked away, a little dark and feels as if you have found your very own hidey-hole away from the world. A word of warning: the only seats are on the tatami—ask for extra cushioning if you don't have your own!

Things liven up a little in the evening, so stick around for a glass of wine at a French-sounding café or bar and soak up the vibe as the lights go down on this entrancing hill. ●

ASAKUSA & KAPPABASHI

Asakusa & Kappabashi

N

Kototoi Dori

Kokusai Dori

Kappabashi

Kaminarimon Dori

Orange Street

Asakusa Dori

KURAMAE
↓

Asakusa Station

Tawaramachi Station

Asakusa has always been a favourite part of Tokyo for me. Although an ever-popular precinct for the Japanese, who attend the rich and colourful festivals held here throughout the year, for a long time it didn't really feature on the average foreign tourist's route. I loved the once comparative remoteness in Tokyo's northeastern corner but, as happens all too frequently in the Big Sushi, things have changed.

Savvy travellers swarm daily to the almighty Sensooji—also known as Asakusa Kannon Temple. They come via its striking Kaminarimon (God of Thunder) gate and eternally buzzing Nakamise shopping arcade, which leads all the way up to the heart of the temple. The original structure, built in 645 in honour of the Buddhist deity Kannon, makes the temple the oldest in Tokyo—even the shopping street has a history of several centuries.

Try to avoid the crowds by going very early or later in the day. It is rather lovely in the evening when lit up to a glowing vermilion. In the covered arcades besides Nakamise you'll find extensive shopping opportunities for a mix of gimmicky and perfect souvenirs and keepsakes. However, in the quieter streets behind the main part of the temple, you'll discover copious amounts of wa-mono (traditional Japanese goods), matsuri (festival) wear and paraphernalia, hand-beaten copper pots and kettles, Edo-period-style cut-glass whisky tumblers and sake glasses, and other items crafted by generations of fascinating artisan families—and the odd cautious shopkeeper character too.

Nearby **Kappabashi** is a long strip of shops catering to food businesses, and now equally crowded with tourists who have caught on to the low prices of quality items. Store after store is filled to the rafters with those famous wax food replicas you see in restaurant windows, plus a vast selection of ceramics, pots, pans, knives and the like, suitable for traditional and contemporary cuisine. My hot tip to you—buy and post home! Japan post is secure, fast and affordable.

In the backstreets of the town there is still an authentic neighbourhood spirit. It's here I simply like to wander with my camera, capturing people going about their daily routine, facades of weather-worn and emotive architecture and intimate street details, which may or may not be there on my return. It's the heart and soul of the area.

SUGGESTED WALK

Several train lines serve **Asakusa Station** ⊖. No matter which exit you take, it's just a couple of minutes' walk to the **Kaminarimon Gate** ❶, which is well signposted.

Standing with the gate behind you, look across the road just a little to the left to the handsome **Asakusa Cultural Information Centre** ❷, designed by Kengo Kuma (*see* Akagi Jinja p185). Only opened in 2012, this is a great resource for area guides, maps, free Wi-Fi and clean toilets—plus there's an excellent view from the eighth floor.

If you really want to look like a tourist—and let's face it, you won't be alone so why not risk embarrassment for a fun photo op—there's an abundance of rickshaws in the area with purposely handsome drivers, some of whom speak a little English. There's always a plentiful supply in front of the **Kaminarimon Gate** ❶.

Push your way past the selfie-stick-wielding crowds, through the gate and into **Nakamise** ❸ (meaning middle shops)—an open-air pathway lined either side with stalls leading all the way to the main temple hall of **Sensooji** ❿.

Japanese sweets and senbei (rice crackers), souvenirs, postcards, kimono and yukata (summer kimono), traditional masks, stylish carry bags, fans and lots of fun Japanese novelty items provide more than adequate souvenir purchasing opportunities. There are several open sections along the way to make a quick escape if the crowds just get too much.

If you do decide to zip off to the side, you'll notice the shopkeeper access lanes that run behind the Nakamise shops—all have matching rust-red doors and awnings. Directly opposite are even more shops, mainly selling items somehow connected to Japanese culture and festival wear—hair ornaments and combs, neat clutches, slip-on silk

shoes for kimono and the like. Jutting off these long lanes are many more little arcades or alleys with, you guessed it, even more places to spend money—or make a pit stop for refreshments.

Some of the arcades are particularly daggy but there are a few gems to be found. I have a couple of favourite shops on the eastern side of Nakamise, to which I always return. The easiest way to find them is to turn right at the second break in the Nakamise strip into a covered arcade.

On your left you'll see **Kanzashiya Wargo** ❹—a shop selling modern hair accessories based on Japanese traditional materials and styles. Right next door is **Kuriko-an** ❺, famous for taikyaki— fish-shaped pancakes filled with sweet red beans and custard cream. Shortly after you'll pass **Kineya** ❻, a much-revered senbei (rice cracker) store, if you're in need of snacks for your in-room private sake party.

Take the next laneway left and you'll come to **Kiryudo** ❼, which specialises in kimono accessories—glorious silk ties and fasteners for obi (wide kimono sashes), bags, purses and the like. They have a few crafty items made from offcuts, which make well-priced, unique and decorative gifts. A few doors up on the same side is **Haneda** ❽, owned by the same people as Kiryudo, but this shop contains an eclectic, fun and stylish range of zakka (miscellaneous knick-knack décor), including hanging decorations and the most extravagantly packaged toilet paper you could imagine.

Reconnecting to **Nakamise** ❸ will have you back on track and bypassing much of the throng. You will go through another large gate with lanterns, **Hozomon Gate** ❾, before you near the main hall, **Sensooji** ❿, which was destroyed in the Second World War and then reconstructed. Directly before the hall is a large bronze urn where people place incense sticks as they pray and direct the plumes of

healing smoke over ailing body parts. Even balding men rub the smoke into their craniums in hope of new growth. The sticks can be purchased at various spots close by for those who are curious. Spend some time exploring the temple grounds. Look for Buddha's giant straw sandals, calm-inspiring statues and places to buy and hang ema (votifs) and omukuji (fortunes) to help your prayers and wishes come true.

You won't be able to miss a whitish tower in the distance to the east—more accurately a 'very pale indigo' to blend into the sky. This is the **Tokyo Skytree** ⓫. The 643-metre high broadcasting tower not only boasts two observation deck levels with views across the mega-metropolis—but many floors of contemporary, popular retail outlets and restaurants (several with English menus). It's a polished one-stop shopping venue with something for everyone. If you have kids in tow, there's an aquarium, a planetarium and cute 'n quirky NHK TV character toys to take home. The Oshiage train station is in the basement and it is a quick ride from **Asakusa Station** 🚇. If you are staying for a few days and inclement weather hampers your plans for wandering around outdoors, this is a good place to eat up a few hours.

... one of the few things that survived the bombings of the Second World War— an important but quiet monument for generations of locals.

Just east of the main temple hall you'll find a smaller hall and that of the **Asakusa Shrine** ⓬. It's perhaps a little confusing to see a Shinto shrine within a Buddhist temple, but this is common, as the Japanese follow both their indigenous Shinto religion and adopted Buddhism—or at very least the rituals and celebrations apportioned to each. Built in 1649, the shrine is one of the few buildings in the area to have survived the bombings of the Second World War.

Just south of the shrine you'll find a tree stump with significant, but little known history. It too stands, hollowed out by fire, as one of the few things that survived the bombings of the Second World War—an important but quiet monument for generations of locals. Most people who visit bustling, happy **Sensooji** ❿ do so unaware of the serious and sad history of the area. It was also once a shitamachi (directly translated as 'down town'), a poor area where the 'common' folk lived, complete with a red-light district.

When I recently learned more about the area from an older friend, whose family has lived here for many generations, I began to understand why I've always felt so connected to the energy. It is indeed palpable—especially if you cover your eyes and ears. They say the locals in the area are a bit precious about maintaining their privacy and old-school ways, and they are not fond of tourists, but I've only come up against mild angst on occasion, now completely justified—there's a long and complex history here.

If you head out of the gate you'll find a building on your left housing the **AMUSE Museum** ⓲ and its outstanding shop of Japanese arts and crafts. The museum hosts a range of cultural exhibitions, including both traditional and contemporary collections, and houses a permanent ukiyo-e print theatre. I was deeply thrilled to witness one of the best and most informative (semi-permanent) displays of boro in Japan in their main exhibition space. Boro is folk

13

fabric once utilised by peasants, artisans and farmers, and made
of sewn-together rags of natural tones, predominantly indigo, in
the strong Japanese spirit of mottainai (waste not) to make clothing,
rugs, blankets and even nappies. An additional extra is the 'gallery
market', where young artists and craftspersons' works are also
displayed and on sale. A relatively well-kept secret is the spectacular
view from the sixth-floor roof and its **Bar Six** 🄬, which opens at night.

If you keep walking to the corner of the main street and take a
left, just a few shops up is **Marble** 🄯, a ninety-year-old handmade-
brush shop: hair, make-up, shaving, body/shower, nail, paint—you
name it! Plus handcrafted brooms of various lengths for a range of
purposes, and ostrich-feather dusters.

Return to the main hall of **Sensooji** 🄼, with it on your right, and
turn right at the corner of the building. You will be in front of the
western wall, where young ladies in kimono like to take photos of

themselves against the giant vermilion doors. Directly opposite this is a small park and koi pond with a bridge—walk over it. You'll note another smaller temple building on your right, and then a small shrine on your left.

Shortly after, you'll walk under a gateway to a small street of touristy shops. Trot past **Hanayashiki** 🔟, a famous old amusement park, until you arrive at the entrance to an old-school shotengai (shopping arcade) on your right, full of basic everyday necessities.

Walk through to the northern exit and you'll find yourself in area rarely visited by foreigners. If you have plenty of time and feel like wandering where the real folk are around here, then cross the road (Kototoi Dori) and continue strolling past the stores. On the corner of the fourth cross street, note the third-generation doki-ya (copper shop) **Asakusa Dougin Douki** 🔟 on your left. It sells beautifully hand-beaten copper and silver teapots, sake warmers, frying pans and nabe (hotpots). Mostly, I love people-watching around here, as it feels like stepping back in time.

Mostly, I love people-watching around here as it feels like stepping back in time.

If you happen to find yourself hungry on your jaunt, seek out **Carbo** 🔟—a pasta joint specialising in delicious Japanified carbonara. You pay via machine as you do at ramen shops, and your lunch and a glass of wine—for less than 1000 yen—are at your table almost as soon as you sit down! An unlikely spot in this traditional area, but this fun concept is a refreshing random interjection.

If you are after something sweet or savoury in the baked goods department, check out **Sekine Bakery** 🔟, an old-fashioned Japanese/German-style bäckerei in the same street, next to the quaint Café Danke. At least take a peek through their windows at the buns with super-cute faces!

Duck 150 metres east of the shotengai to find **Meugaya** 🔟. Established in the 1800s, it specialises in festival wear, including gorgeous tabi (split-toe socks) and the cutest, tiniest kids' kimono you ever did see.

泉滴（税込）
円型 ¥10500
タル型 ¥13650

¥18360

17

18

22

Let's return to the northern mouth of the arcade; continue west for about 400 metres until you hit **Kappabashi** ㉑. Look out for the green and yellow mythical lizard/bird-like Kappa face staring at you from the signposts to ensure you are in the right place.

Kappabashi, taking up almost a kilometre of a much longer boulevard, is lined on each side with wholesale restaurant and catering equipment, which is also open to the public. Kicked off by just a handful of merchants around 1912, the well-known area covers everything from the finest-quality chef's knives and commercial kitchen appliances to attractive dinnerware including a notable array of cheap Japanese ceramics and lacquerware. I like **Nishiyama's** ㉒ for lacquerware bowls and trays and **Kamata** ㉓ for dreamy knives. Remember Japanese post is extremely efficient, quick and cheap—buy up and ship them home so you don't blow your luggage allowance.

Even if you're not into cooking or tableware, you'll likely be mesmerised by the handful of shops specialising in realistic imitation foods used in Japanese restaurant windows to display menu items. It's hard to resist grabbing a small one to take home and show off to your friends. The real deal are expensive but, being Japan, there are of course some gift items, such as life-sized sushi fridge magnets and bacon rasher bookmarks. Head to **Maizuru** 24 for high-quality wax food models.

It is quite a long road, and unless you are truly dedicated to kitting out your kitchen you might like to take one of the streets off to your left. All left turns off the east side of the street pretty much lead you back to **Sensooji** 10 via plenty more souvenir shops—some more interesting than others. Keep an eye out for a couple of artisan stores on 'Orange Street'. **Asakusa Maekawa Tsurushi Shuto** 25 focuses on wallets, bags and accessories made only from authentic deer leather (tsurushi shuto), printed with a fine Japanese lacquer

in traditional patterns. Beware: there are many cheap imitations around town—most recognisable to the novice by the price difference. **Asakusa Mori Gin** ㉖ specialises in traditional silversmith items, including netsuke-inspired jewellery, sake cups, belt buckles, chopsticks and their rests.

If you've been seriously looking along the length of **Kappabashi** ㉑, you'll notice there are several giant kitchen-centric items on some rooftops, including a whisk, a giant knife and a Kappa—the street mascot. If you reach as far south as the Niimi building topped with the giant chef's head on Asakusa Dori, you've come about as far as you need to on this street.

Take a left into Asakasa Dori, walk past Tawaramachi Station, then take the next left onto the wide Kokusai Dori, just after the post office. If it happens to be around the dinnertime mark, Asakusa is famous for tempura. I can highly recommend a top-notch but reasonably priced casual tempura restaurant right about where you will be standing—**Tempura Takenawa** ㉗. It is close to exit 3 of Tawaramachi Station. Pristine seafood and vegetables feature in a well-seasoned, ultra-crisp batter. They also have excellent sashimi platters to kick things off, with perfect chawan mushi (steamed savoury custard) to end.

Keep walking north for four short blocks, and then turn right into Kaminarimon Dori. You're a few minutes away from being back at the front of **Kaminarimon Gate** ❶, where you started your day.

You could easily spend a second day wandering all the little laneways between the main arteries of shopping arcades. You could also visit nearby Kuramae (p218), an up-and-coming area for design goods, stylish homewares and fashions only moments away from the heart of Asakusa.

If you are sticking around, I recommend **The Gate Hotel** ㉘ (p271) by Hulic. It's a great way to make sure you experience the temple area in the evening, when it is quiet and atmospheric under the striking lanterns and strategically lit pagodas. The glowing vermilion provides a sense of warmth, especially on a cool night. First thing in the morning is also a particularly peaceful time to visit. ⬤

KURAMAE, OKACHIMACHI, AKIHABARA & KANDA-OCHANOMIZU

Kuramae, Okachimachi, Akihabara & Kanda-Ochanomizu

Shin Okachimachi Station

16

Tsukuba Express

13

15

14

Kokusai Dori

5

Edo Dori

4

2

3

7

6

8

1

Kuramae Station

12

10

9

11

Sumida River

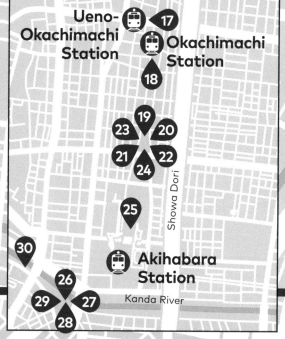

Ueno-Okachimachi Station

17

Okachimachi Station

18

19

23

20

21

22

24

25

Showa Dori

30

Akihabara Station

26

29

27

28

Kanda River

This jumble of sharp-sounding suburbs might seem like more than a mouthful for one day, but the key points of these connecting areas are easily traversed. They provide many, but not an overwhelming amount, of extremely enjoyable and quirky shopping experiences, and wonderful photographic opportunities.

Kuramae, just one stop south of Asakusa (p194) Station on the Asakusa line, is a charming pocket of Tokyo. It blossoms by day, with creative spaces housing up-and-coming designers and local craftspeople who are confidently and respectfully adding a young and fashionable edge on tradition.

Within strolling distance to the west is **Okachimachi**, and the peaceful streets between the two promise an earthy, surprising and delightful wander.

The old-school architecture and local village food-shopping street of Okazu Yokocho are reason enough for the aesthetician in you to visit. However, you won't get away from this part of town without several carry bags of 'I can't live without this' kinda gear.

Fresh concepts combined with considered, superior craftsmanship make it all extremely desirable. In the vein of New York's SoHo and Tribeca, the affectionate collective name for the area is Kachikura (**Okachi**machi/**Kura**mae).

Near Shin Okachimachi Station, in the northern part of the precinct, is the Taito Designers Village—no doubt heavily responsible for the growth of captivating shops in this area. An expanding café scene and youth-savvy accommodation seem to be encouraging the movement.

South of Okachimachi and southwest of Kuramae is a newish design precinct, quietly referred to as Aki-Oka (**Aki**habara/**Oka**chimachi). This is a must-visit before you arrive at neon-powered **Akihabara** electric town—an unlikely addition to this guide due to its reputation as otaku (nerd) gamer central. However, en route to the **Kanda-Ochanomizu** area, you simply must pass through this energising quarter—where you'll find a great new Japanese food store called Chabara (o**cha**nomizu/akiha**bara**), before arriving at Maach e cute in a now-defunct railway station, slap bang between Kanda and Ochanomizu stations.

These up-and-coming areas boast intimate 'design and detail' shopping and dining precincts, which glisten in their own slick of Tokyo underground style—or 'under-track style' as the case may be—almost hidden in the shadows. Some of the best things about Japan are those that are not entirely obvious. If you have an eye for something a little out of the box, you'll fall in love with this part of Tokyo.

SUGGESTED WALK

This route covers a bit of terrain, so feel free to jump on a train or hail a taxi to give you a break. Still, it's all doable in a day and sets you up for dinner at either end, should you reverse the route.

Leave via the east exit of **Kuramae Station** 🚇 and cross Edo Dori in the direction of the Sumida River. You'll see the Kuramae outlet of **Koncent** ❶—a contemporary design store of innovative stationery items. Some border on 'just plain silly but a whole lotta fun'—and all promise to spruce up your office space, home or life in one way or another.

Turn right out of the store and head up Edo Dori, taking the third street on your right. Head towards the river for a few minutes, but turn left at the third street—if you hit the water you've gone too

far. Almost straight away you'll see **Nui** ❷—a popular backpackers' hostel and bar on your left. The vibe is bohemian and laid back.

Diagonally across the way is a colourful riverside café—**Cielo y Rio** ❸—a relaxed place for a mid-morning fuel stop of caffeine and cake or an early lunch. Stop and plan your attack on this area, which is more sparsely set out than others. (If you do this walk in reverse, it's not a bad spot for dinner after you've had a drink at **Nui** ❷.)

Continue along to the doorway of **New Old Stock by Otogi** ❹ by Otogi Designs—a tiny antique, design and accessory store where you need to breathe in just to squeeze between the closely packed displays. There are trinkets and treasures to be found if you are patient—check out their very own colourful casual-soft-shoe range.

Further up a rickety stairwell is a creative space that hosts regular workshops for handmade decorative items for the house and garden. If you make it down the stairs alive, keep walking until you reach

In-Kyo ❺—a small, traditionally inspired homewares/lifestyle shop with predominantly kitchenware, pots and some books. It is a little austere service-wise, but they have a few elegant items worth peeking at, and the store itself has a lovely feel.

From In-Kyo, walk in a westerly direction about 350 metres to wide Kokusai Dori. Turn left and follow the road south. After about seven streets, turn left if you are in the market for beautiful handcrafted wallets, totes, satchels, cases and other miscellaneous items dyed with natural products in earthy tones. At **M+** ❻, most of the range has a slightly masculine feel but is ultimately unisex.

Return to Kokusai Dori and cross the road to find **Maito** ❼ a few steps south—a business centred on organic dyed yarn and gorgeous knitwear. They also run workshops on natural plant dyeing. Two streets south of Maito, turn right and almost immediately on your right is **REN** ❽—for the most spectacularly soft yet durable handmade leather bags, wallets, card cases and tablet covers. These are predominantly made from pig, cow or goat skins and tinted with a wide variety of natural hues. Divine. The indigo canvas and soft wool bags are also fabulous. I want one of everything. Between M+ and Ren I could kit myself out for the next few decades.

Continue on this street, passing **CC4441 ❾** on your left—a small gallery space constructed of shipping containers—then turn left at the next set of traffic lights. After a couple of short blocks you will find my favourite store in this area, **SYU-RO ❿**, on the right. It's stocked with a wonderland's worth of 'monozukuri'—handmade creativity from all over Japan. Paper-thin copper, brass and tinplate tea canisters—use them for any small items—indigo sacks, Okinawan throws, soap and cloth, onion-skin paper notebooks, smooth-as-silk wooden boxes. Note that it doesn't open till 12 pm.

It's stocked with a wonderland's worth of 'monozukuri'—handmade creativity from all over Japan.

When you exit the shop—inevitably laden with presents to self—continue to the next corner and turn right, walking under the sign-posted entranceway to **Okazu Yokocho ⓫** (side dish alley). It was established in the 1950s and was once lined with, as the name suggests, shops selling side dishes such as tsukudani (seaweed, fish and dried vegetables preserved in sweetened soy), grilled fish, and vegetables—simmered or pickled. Locals could also find daily groceries, such as miso or soba noodles. This made light work for busy homemakers back in the Meiji period (1868–1912), when industry was taking off and often both husband and wife were working and could afford a little help in the kitchen. You could think of it as an old-time version of a convenience store—only offering much healthier, higher-quality foodstuffs.

Today, there are still many rustic stalls mixed with more contemporary vendors selling an eclectic collection of goods, from fresh vegetables and sushi to folksy ceramics, Japanese tea and wagashi (traditional tea sweets), grilled chicken and eel, cashmere scarves and intricately hand-woven jewellery. The atmosphere is terrific, particularly on a Saturday, when there are often pop-up

handicraft stores, too. *Most shops are closed on a Sunday*. Explore the whole strip and the richly atmospheric and utterly photogenic streets that run perpendicular and parallel to the Yokocho. To get you started, here are a couple of places of note.

Firstly, **Tsubamekobo** ⓬ is a surprise sweetie bag of a shop run by a friendly wife and husband team. Kyoko Takahashi is a textile artist who makes the most beautifully delicate hand-woven scarves and the like from natural fibres such as cashmere and linen. Be sure to cast your eyes over her brilliant sea-anemone-like brooches and unique earrings covered in thread.

If there is a market on at the **Taito Designers Village** ⓭ it is worth taking a sidestep towards the low-rent studio space set up inside an old, unused primary school. The space was established to support young, aspiring designers of fashion and related products. When the potentially famous tenants host a market to display and move on their wares, it's a top spot for bargains on one-off clothing, jewellery and accessories. To get there—walk a few metres past **Tsubamekobo** ⓬ just under another metal archway.

Take a right here and keep walking until the end of the street, then make a dogleg right and an immediate left. Continue until you come to a couple of great little zakka—miscellaneous and fun design goods stores—**BRASS** ⓮ and **Carmine** ⓯, with their fantastic origami-inspired purses. On exiting Carmine, walk straight ahead (north) and on your right you will spot the **Taito Designers Village** ⓭.

Keep going to the main road—Tsukuba Expressway—and turn left. You will shortly be in front of **Shin Okachimachi Station** ⓰. Take the Oedo line one stop to the **Ueno-Okachimachi Station** ⓱, then walk 3 minutes to adjacent **Okachimachi Station** ⓲. I know, so much Okachimachi. Take a street either side of the tracks and walk for about 400 metres south until **2k540 Aki-Oka Artisan** ⓳—a wondrously stylish and cool under-track young designer shopping precinct.

If the train thing is too hard, show a taxi driver the Aki-Oka address. Or the phone number—they can always look up a business that way and prefer it to the written address sometimes. Or just say 'Okachimachi eki' (station) if they look too confused! You'll recognise the place from its white shipping-container-like shop structures, which almost downplay the truly cool shopping area that it is. So Japanese.

If you bypass **Taito Designers Village** ⓭ and head directly to
2k540 Aki-Oka Artisan ⓳ from **Tsubamekobo** ⓬, you simply need
to walk about 100 metres west to the end of the Okazu Yokocho
alley, then take a left into Kiyosou Bashi Dori to the main road,
Kuramae-hashi Dori. Turn right (west) and follow it for about 600
metres. Walk under the expressway and Aki-Oka is straight ahead on
your right. Personally, I'd save your feet and grab a taxi, as there's
still a lot of walking and shopping to do.

The Aki-Oka space feels like what I imagine an elongated
design-college dorm with an open door policy would be. You'll want
to dart in and out as creative forms catch your eye. No doubt, some
quality time will be spent exploring the shops that most appeal.

Look out for **The Nippon Department store** ⓴. You might want to
buy the shop out of their traditionally inspired design stock—gorgeous
cushions, dolls and handcrafted goods from all over the country.

Hacoa 21 specialises in handsome wood versions of everyday stuff —stationery, keyboards, smartphone stands, plus smoothly polished brooches and watches—all made in Hokkaido in northern Japan.

Studio Uamou 22 is the gallery shop of artist Ayako Takagi. Poke your head in to meet her small, vinyl creature characters—uamou, boo and bastard. Her brother runs the laid-back adjacent café/bar too.

Nakazawa 23 is for carry-bag addicts with elegant to obscure taste. Check out their quirky penguin or phone handbags.

At **Tokyo Noble 24** you can also commission a custom-made brolly in a choice of seventy-seven different UV-filtering fabrics—the vegetable print umbrellas are my favourite.

Please note that most stores are closed on Wednesdays.

Head out the southeast side exit and walk south towards Akihabara Station for about 400 metres. At the third set of traffic lights, take a right under the tracks, then an immediate right and you'll be standing

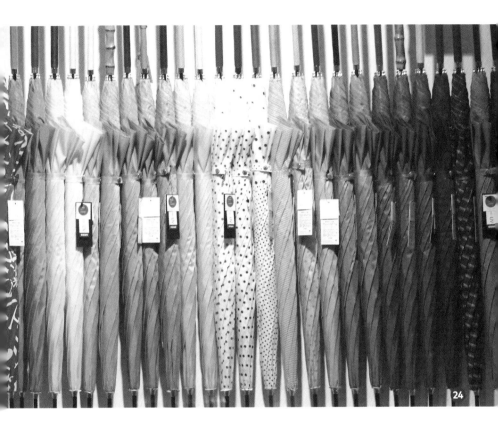

24

outside **Chabara** ㉕. Related to **Aki-Oka** ⑲—both the brainchildren of Japan Railways and a successful attempt to make better use of the under-rail space—this fascinating foodie's paradise is packed with regional specialty ingredients and foodstuffs from the tip to toe of Japan. Finds include sake, wine, tea, snacks and ice cream. It's a must-see if you're interested in Japanese cookery or culinary culture.

Take the southwest corner exit out of Chabara, turn right onto Chuo Dori and walk 100 metres to intersection. If it's twilight or later, you won't be able to miss the neon circus of Akihabara's electric town along this strip—worth a look just to experience something you won't see in any other place in the world.

It's truly an 'in your face' part of town—and if you fade away at the thought of overstimulation or are sensitive to flickering lights and fluorescent scenes, you'll be scurrying right through this section, dodging the maid café vendors.

26

¥37,800—

26

29

Head left across the road and after about 300 metres cross the bridge over the Kanda River. On your right is **Maach e cute** ㉖, a splendid little open-plan shopping centre of mainly Japanese design goods in the defunct Kanda Manseibashi train station.

If you're feeling parched I have two excellent suggestions. **The Hitachino Brewing Lab** ㉗—look for the owl motif—is a local craft beer specialist. However, if you are a trainspotter or armchair thrill-seeker, head to **N331** ㉘ on the second floor at the opposite end of the building. This glassed-in café and bar sits on what was the old train platform, situated between two still very much working train lines. It's a magnificent spot to sit, refreshment in hand, watching the trains clitter-clattering past in muffled tones as the sun sinks into the land beyond the skyscrapers.

Once refreshed, take a relaxed and leisurely stroll through the ground-floor, creative market-like shopping space—yet another of

those venues where you'll sense a desire to walk away with a little something to add to your shopping haul.

Conveniently, **Fukumori** 29 includes both a shop and Japanese/Scandi-vibed blonde-wood café with views of the river. My kind of shopping. If it's the end of the day there are plenty of bars and restaurants on the outer edge of the building, which faces away from the river. If your feet can stand it, there are even more eateries at nearby **Ochanomizu Brick Mall** 30—underneath another part of the tracks. Then, pop yourself in a taxi and get some well-earned rest. ●

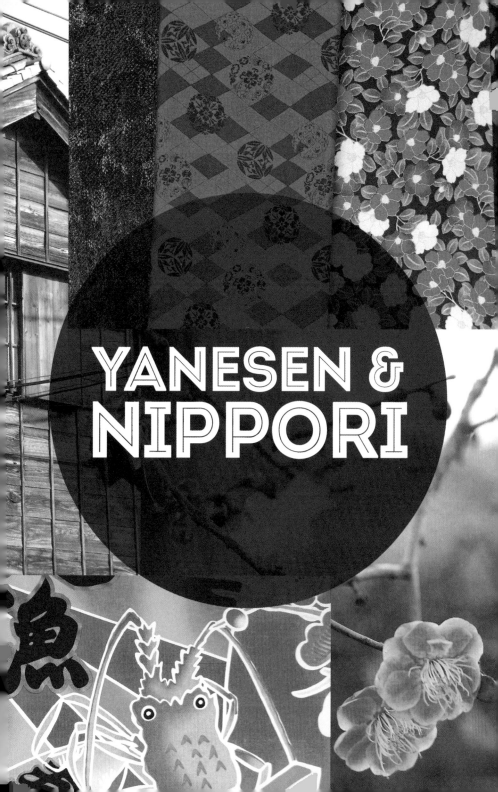

YANESEN & NIPPORI

Yanesen & Nippori

Nippori Station

Yanaka Cemetery

Kototoi Dori

If you've made it this far, you've broken through Tokyo's shining patina into its crust. Once you've entered the mystery and magic of the 'real' Japan, you'll want to keep digging. There's just so much to see and do in this historical yet style-conscious vault of a city.

Yanesen is the collective name for a quaint district that hugs together three 'shitamachi' or downtown neighbourhoods: Yanaka, Nezu and Sendagi. Incredible traditional buildings still line the streets, having fortuitously survived both the Great Kanto Earthquake of 1923 and the action of the Second World War. These buildings provide the backdrop to a strong village culture with a clear sense of connectedness.

Its well-known cemetery Yanaka Reien is surprisingly pleasant to stroll through due to the tunnel of sakura (cherry blossom) trees that line its wide pathways. History buffs may appreciate that the tomb of Japan's last Shogun, Yoshinobu Tokugawa (1837–1913), is housed here. He rests alongside many other important historical figures, famous artists, writers and actors, who lend considerable 'cred' to the local community, which thrives on culture, history, creativity and authenticity.

The cemetery backs right up against Ueno—a stupendously busy part of town— yet Yanaka retains the atmosphere of a quiet, faraway suburb. A significant cluster, in advance of 100, aged Buddhist temples provide an aesthetic and energy that are akin to those of the ancient capital Kyoto.

The action of course (and there is always action in Tokyo town) centres around an Edo-period (1603–1867) shopping street called Yanaka Ginza. However, it's in the tentacles that run off the main artery that a quietly encompassing beauty lures the deeply curious and tuned-in for long walks of discovery. You can dip in and out of antique stores and temples, galleries, craft shops and cosy cafés. The number of artists and creatives who are attracted to the area, and their businesses that continue to launch in back streets, are testament to the inherent air of inspiration and intrigue.

Some of the older shopkeepers along the main strip are a bit protective and can be uncharacteristically rude, but that is honestly part of Yanesen's charm. It is indicative of the locals' deep respect for tradition and desire to keep things from growing into a high-rise, commercial hub—and you really can't knock that, especially in a city that constantly morphs and grows, demolishes and rebuilds. Yanesen has become a bit of a tourist hub for its differences— particularly for those seeking a deeper travel experience.

Nippori, just north of Yanesen, is a neighbourhood that also runs at a slower pace, except for one long street known as Senigai, or fabric town. It bustles with doting obaachan (grannies) and nimble-fingered crafty types in search of bargains in fabric, buttons, ribbons and thread.

SUGGESTED WALK

You'll feel like you are snaking around a bit on this trail, but it's really the only way to see the highlights. Yanaka is the central point for this itinerary, which barely skims the edges of Nezu and Sendagi. If you have time, come back another day and explore further.

Leave the upper level of the west exit of **Nippori Station** ⊖ and walk up the slight incline. Within a few steps you'll find a small corner of Tennoji Temple's graveyard on your left, and Hongyotera

(temple) on your right. Just after the temple are basic, everyday goods stores in slightly run-down yet attractive buildings.

Presenting soon on your left will be the handsome **Yanaka Senbei Shinsendo ❶** shop, founded in 1913. Its counter top is covered with bulbous glass jars filled with delicious, freshly made savoury and sweet rice crackers. You'd be wise to pick up a packet or two for in-room drinks. You can't say I don't look after you.

If you keep walking straight ahead you'll see a small building at the apex of a fork in the road. Take the street on the right. Some days there will be a handful of stallholders in this vicinity, and on weekends a significant number of people mill around, so you may need to push through them to locate the stairs down to **Yanaka Ginza ❷**. At the bottom of the stairs is a triangular peaked archway that marks the entrance to the shopping strip. On either side is a mix of stalls selling traditional fresh foods, tea and Japanese confectionery, dotted with more contemporary stores touting reasonably mundane fashion items and accessories. You'll notice queues at a couple of the food shops famous for their yakitori or minchi katsu (mince croquettes). Follow those in-the-know noses to treat yourself—possibly in more ways than one. Did you ever see that 'Soup Nazi' episode on *Seinfeld*? I'll leave it at that.

Take time to admire the contemporary black-and-white woodblock print artwork adorning walls above the shops—each depicts scenes from the neighbourhood. While you are looking up, you might also spy a certain predilection towards the feline species along the awning tops—a nod to the high concentration of temple cat strays in the area. On a sunny day you'll notice them basking on gravestones or wandering among the flowerpots.

Although I enjoy the slightly frenetic, jovial mood and general dagginess of this strip, there is just a handful of businesses I like to drop into before moving on to more interesting parts of Yanesen:

Hankoya Shinimonogurui ❸ for famously cheeky 'hanko' (personal seal stamps)—the popular artwork has extended to wearable merchandise.

Yakikarintou ❹ for crisp sweets with Japanese black–brown sugar coating—the ume (plum) version is unique.

Motherhouse ❺ for handcrafted leather and jute bags and accessories, and naturally dyed wraps in organic knit fabrics.

Niku no Suzuki ❻ for old-school yoshoku ('western') snack food korokke (croquettes)—try the kani (crab) cream and famous minchi katsu (beef and potato) flavours.

Atom bakery ❼ for delicious Japanese oyatsu pan (snack breads seasoned or filled with all manner of delicious ingredients), baked in an oven made of volcanic rock from Mount Fuji. The shop is named after the cartoon character Atom, or Astro Boy as we know him, and decorated accordingly. That's Tokyo!

Kanekichien ❽ for quality Japanese tea and related accoutrements. You'll naturally require a pretty canister or teapot that respects the fine, aromatic cha you are inevitably going to purchase.

Waguriya ❾ for traditional and modern takes on sweets made from the finest-quality chestnuts, including the eternally popular Mont Blanc—a combination of sweetened chestnut puree and the purest of cream.

At the end of the shotengai, turn right and a few buildings along on the right is the **Yanesen Centre ❿**. This is the local tourist and culture information centre. Grab a map in English to help you explore further afield on your own.

I f you have ample time up your sleeve and are in the mood for a nature break, turn left out of the information centre and continue walking through an extension of neighbourhood charm—cheery fishmongers, antique kimono stores and the odd café. In about 200 metres you will be close to Sendagi Station and in 600 metres you'll reach **Nezu Jinja ⓫**—one of Japan's oldest shrines. Its sprawling gardens are famous for their Azalea Festival in May and the photogenic tunnels of vermilion torii (shrine gates) that line certain pathways. You might want to hop in a taxi for this one!

However, if you are still following me, retrace your path back through **Yanaka Ginza ❷** and up the stairs. Take the first right after the fork in the road you passed on the way down. You'll immediately start to notice some older buildings with loads of character, and perhaps some artistic types seeking style and substance.

After a block you'll come to the **Asakura Choso ⓬** sculpture museum in an unusual, charcoal-grey structure, with a male sculpture

朝倉彫塑館

14

crouching on the roof peering down at you. It was designed as a residence and studio both for and by the 'father of modern Japanese sculpture', Fumio Asakura (1883–1964). He is particularly famous for his work with bronze. The museum space itself has become popular with architecture students, who come to admire and learn from the unique design—both modern for its time in parts and steadfastly traditional in others. The house was built around a beautiful garden, purposely designed to show off the best of each season.

Close by you'll see **Kaizoin** ⑬, just one of numerous temples you'll pass in this area—many of them relocated from other Tokyo precincts during the Edo period to avoid destruction by the fires that were raging in the heavily overpopulated and quickly growing capital city. It's a peaceful place to take a few moments out and recharge your Zen.

If you take the next right you will find **Choanji Temple** ⑭ on your left, and what is estimated to be a thirteenth-century bluestone wall

on your right. It was originally erected in this temple-dense area as a form of stupa board, or resting place, for deceased souls. Keep following the wall and you'll come to yet another temple on your right. **Kanoin** ⑮ is detectable from its deep-red gate.

Take a right at the next corner and walk to the end of the street, then take a left through a residential laneway until you hit a cross street. Turn right and on the corner of the next street is an eye-catching black building, **HAGISO** ⑯. This is an exhibition space for local artists, with a cosy café—and the perfect spot to take a lunch break if your timing is right. The small but well-executed menu offers simple, lovingly prepared contemporary yoshoku (Japanese–western) dishes, and a cheery selection of hot and cold drinks. The organic-looking homemade cakes and bumper jars of fruit soaking in booze set the scene for kicking back and restoring body, mind and soul.

17

If you're in need of fresh air, there is a park across the road on the ruins of the home built for artist and philosopher Okakura Tenshin (1863–1913). He founded the Tokyo Fine Arts School—now Tokyo University of the Arts.

Turn around and walk south along this residential street for about 200 metres, until you hit a main road. Cross it and turn right. A block or so down on your left you'll see **Isetatsu** 🔟. Founded in 1864, it's well worth the detour for the kimono-pattern-inspired chiyogami— eye-catching woodblock-printed papers for use in decoration, origami or stationery products.

Just two buildings back is **Biscuit** 🔞—a sweet little store of zakka (fun miscellaneous goods), such as antique and retro toys, buttons, colourful ribbons and contemporary paper stationery products.

Walk up the hill for about 300 metres and several small temples later you'll come to a set of traffic lights. Take a quick left and you'll

18

spot **Gate of Life ⑲** on your right. This funky little knick-knack shop
sells a handful of the kind of retro items you'd want to steal from
your Japanese grandmother's house, mingled with retro-inspired
handcrafted contemporary home and fashion accessories.

Further along is **Antique Hatsune ⑳**. Look to your right for
the little gateway with a tiled roof and a wooden gate, fronted by
cobblestones and a healthy pot plant. The breath-taking yet tiny
store is jam-packed. An antique doll collection looks down onto a
jumble of sake cups, kimono boxes, small wooden chests, teapots
and decorative items. You could spend hours sifting through this tiny
treasure trove; tread carefully so as not to rack up extras underfoot.

Across the road is a vibrant-green-tinted Machiya (traditional
merchant house). The downstairs has been renovated by the owner
into a multipurpose community space called **Sankenma ㉑**,
which is used for all sorts of creative activities and workshops, from

shakuhachi flute to handicrafts. If the casual café/bar/exhibition space/shop is hopping, why not pop in?

Double back towards the main road. Cross at the lights to find divine paper and cloth shop **Kamitonuno** ㉒ on your right. On your left is a yellowish building with elaborate ironwork over the windows—walk around the window side and you'll be in front of a tall-for-the-area apartment block. In the basement is **Craft Studio Tokugen** ㉓, a gallery showroom of dangerously exquisite silk clothes and craft, dyed in gradient shades of Japan's famous natural indigo.

Keep walking along the main road, and when you get to the next set of lights you'll see a koban (small police station) on your left and **Scai the Bathhouse** ㉔ on your right. This is home to a small avant-garde gallery that hosts a range of carefully selected, intelligent and intriguing exhibitions. It's worth taking a peek inside the bathhouse

23

25

itself, even if there isn't a showing—just inside the main doors you can see the old lockers still in place.

Should you be up for a wander by even more temples and both beautiful and odd rickety architecture, follow the road the bathhouse is on in a westerly direction and just lose yourself. It really is uplifting and spiritual just to *be* in this old part of town with barely anyone else around.

However, if you are keen to keep moving, walk past the bathhouse until the T-intersection at the next main road, Kototoi Dori. Just before the 'T' on your right is a little group of shops featuring a couple of places to grab a decent coffee. The aromas are intoxicating. Speaking of intoxication, note the small museum to your left—the annex to the **Shitamachi** (down town) **Museum** ㉕ —an Edo-period liquor shop originally stood in this place. It's tiny, and free, and ogle-worthy for the splendid old bottles and posters.

If you continue northeast along this road past the Shitamachi annex to the second set of lights—about 300 metres—you'll see a wide boulevard of old sakura (cherry blossom) trees on your left, sprouting out of green shrubbery squares. A little further up on your left is the popular patisserie and chocolatier **Inamura** 26—just in case the last coffee didn't give you quite the energy kick you needed for the fabric street visit.

Keep following this road into the heart of leafy Yanaka cemetery. It's not everyone's cup of tea to waltz through a cemetery, so spend as much or as little time here as you wish before seeking out one of several signs that lead you back to **Nippori Station** 🚉. If you intend to go on to Nippori Fabric Town, make your way to the east exit and turn right.

To access the main fabric street, head past the large New Tokyo pachinko parlour and cross at the pedestrian crossing to stand in

front of the Ginza Cozy Corner bakery café. Take the street that runs along the left-hand side of the café and at the next set of lights cross to the start of **Nippori Senigai (fabric street)** ㉗—there will be flags or signs along the road to assure you that you're in the right place.

There are many, many shops here, each with their own particular style, so I won't even attempt to guess yours—but I will say there are both elements of tack and sophistication. I'm not proficient with needle and thread, but can't help but be taken with the lengths of fabrics printed with stylised Japanese traditional patterns, since they make cheap-as-chips, attention-attracting tablecloths for home.

The majority of goods are in the first 500 metres. If you have made it to the Edwin building on your left you have probably exhausted all worthy options on this side. Cross the road for closer inspection as you head back to the station. If you are a serious shopper you might just need to lug your haul back in a taxi.

If a visit to Yanesen stirred a need to delve deeper into Japanese traditional art, the **Tokyo National Museum** ㉘ is only a hop, skip and a jump over to neighbouring Ueno. The almost forbidding building in Ueno Park is both a storehouse and showcase for many of Japan's fine-art treasures and antiquities, including significant archaeological finds—plus there's an impressive collection from other parts of Asia, too. ●

PLACES TO STAY

HOTELS

Here's a handful of excellent options with individual personalities, across different parts of the city.

❶ Tokyo Station Hotel, Maranouchi

thetokyostationhotel.jp/

Sitting directly above the magnificent red-brick Tokyo Station building, this superb hotel, which celebrated its one-hundredth birthday in 2015, ticks a whole stack of boxes. Not only would it have to be the most conveniently based hotel in Tokyo, it is rich with history, generously retold by hotel staff, and the beautifully appointed rooms have been recently refurbished in a respectful Meiji-period-inspired (1868–1912) style. If you are sharing with a friend for a few days, invest in the two-storey maisonette rooms and play princesses! But wait, there's more! In a large atrium at the top of the hotel is the most stupendous breakfast room—open only to guests—which offers one of the best buffet breakfasts in the country. Stylish history buffs with a taste for the romantic really cannot go past this hotel, which runs with the kind of precision and friendly service you might expect from the owners of Japan Railways.

❷ Claska, Meguro

claska.com/en/hotel/

Eternally popular with creative types, the Claska Hotel is ideal for those who wish to escape the busier parts of the city in their downtime. There are various room styles, some with one-off interiors designed by local artists. This hotel spans a price range, so it's fair to say there's something for everyone, from the advertising mogul to the frugal artist. If you're staying long term, they have a good deal on their weekly residence rooms, but as there are only a few of this room type available, you need to reserve well in advance. While starting to show signs of age in some parts, the rooms are spacious for Tokyo and the beds wide and comfortable. The Japanese-themed rooms with a contemporary take on traditional style will appeal to the aesthetician with a yen for Zen. The open foyer, restaurant and bar area are the perfect spot in which to relax at any time of the day, or take a drink to the rooftop for spectacular views of Mount Fuji as the sun sets. Even if you don't stay here, make sure you visit hotel shop **Do** (p117) for one of the best selections of Japanese design and décor goods.

❸ Park Hyatt Tokyo, Shinjuku

tokyo.park.hyatt.com/en/hotel/home.html

A stay at the Park Hyatt is quite possibly the quintessential Tokyo Hotel experience. The service is exemplary; you'll be bowled over by their attention to detail. 'Omotenashi', the Japanese word for the highest level of service, which you'll soon realise is an inherent trait throughout the land, is most evident at this beguilingly humble, and in many ways understated, hotel. From the minute you walk through the door until the moment you leave you will be treated like royalty. The rooms are relatively sprawling, with palatial marble bathrooms and top-notch amenities. The beds are bigger than my apartment and the rooms are kitted out with a level of consideration rarely found in a hotel space. Even the mini bar rates a mention for its twinkling selection of sophisticated spirits. It is very expensive but a stay here, even for just one night of your life, is a must-do if you can—

particularly for fans of the movie *Lost in Translation*. If, like me, you've seen it twenty-five times, you'll be pinching yourself sitting in the glamorous fifty-second-floor New York Bar, swaying to live jazz over a dirty martini—all the while imagining Bill or Scarlett are sharing your bar nuts. Make a night of it by having dinner in the romantic **New York Grill**—if you are on your own, the waitstaff will ensure you feel completely comfortable and well looked after. Faultless.

❹ The Gate Hotel by Hulic, Asakusa
gate-hotel.jp/

This well-priced, modern hotel in the traditional downtown and richly atmospheric area of Asakusa is situated almost directly across the road from the famous **Kaminarimon Gate** (p198)—the entrance to the famous Sensooji Temple and surrounds. Their standard rooms, clearly decorated by a fan of the 1980s, are typically compact but

comfortable. Although a little distanced from the centre of the city, it is a doddle to access most parts of town with the train station only metres away. Reception and the restaurant and bar are perched at the top of the hotel, providing the most of the expansive views and putting a little spring into one's step upon every visit to these common areas. The bar's outside deck area is a sublime spot for a cocktail on a clear night over the city lights—and exclusive to hotel guests.

❺ Hotel Metropolitan, Ikebukuro
metropolitan.jp/

While it ain't the cultural epicentre of Tokyo, bustling Ikebukuro is an excellent base for travelling to some of the more interesting outer suburbs, such as Kichijoji and Koenji (p130). The huge, old-school Hotel Metropolitan offers a good alternative to some of the newer, fancier and more expensive Tokyo accommodations. Ideal for families or groups of friends, the clean, comfortable hotel boasts a wide range of drinking and dining options, and just about everything you could possibly need for a fun-packed holiday is situated within close proximity. Mighty shopping complexes and entertainment areas surround the hotel, and Ikebukuro Station is directly across the road. The twenty-fifth-floor bar offers views of Mount Fuji over drinks and snacks. Take advantage of the special sake and food-matching experience in the **Hanamusashi Shunka restaurant**—as you dine, one of their helpful staff explains the nuances of each sake, providing an excellent learning opportunity for those with an interest in the national drop.

❻ The Strings by Intercontinental, Shinagawa
intercontinental-strings.jp/

Located just a couple of minutes' stroll from the bustling Shinagawa Station via an easy-to-locate covered walkway is this stylish hotel on floors twenty-six to thirty-two of a sleek office tower. There are only two shinkansen (bullet train) stops in Tokyo, and Shinagawa Station is home to one of them—the other is situated at Tokyo Station—so if you're travelling on to Kyoto or other cities, both this hotel (and the Tokyo Station Hotel p268) are extremely convenient. However, the well-designed newer Shinagawa Station is easier to navigate than Tokyo Station—and a little less frantic, being just that little bit out of the hustle-bustle of the central city area. For those who wish to explore Tokyo at a slightly slower pace, this hotel is a good option.

But don't let me confuse you, there are still squillions of things to do and see in the area and you're not far from the centre at all. The station itself and the surrounding area house plenty of restaurants and shops. The rooms are comfortable and decorated in relaxing, natural tones, and most offer expansive views of the city. Although subtle, the open lobby and dining area appear to have been planned like a Zen garden, complete with a shallow 'pond' and bridge to the bar and restaurant zones. You'll notice an instant calming, welcoming energy as soon as you enter the hotel.

❼ Granbell Hotels x 3

granbellhotel.jp/en/

The Granbell Hotel Group owns three hotels in Tokyo, all conveniently situated in the entertainment/nightlife hubs of Shibuya, Shinjuku and Akasaka, and within walking distance of major train stations.

They are referred to as 'design' or 'art' hotels. While there are indeed some aspects of art and design within the confines of each building, some rooms are more basic and less styled than others and priced accordingly, so do take time to examine each room type on their website before deciding. Each hotel boasts its own character, but as a group they share compact, clean, functional rooms with comfortable, firm-ish beds and pleasant staff—though not a lot of English is spoken. Although the hotels are situated in busy areas close to heavy traffic and thriving shops, bars and restaurants, the rooms themselves are pin-drop quiet—unless you open the window. On my visit to the Shibuya Granbell, some of the rooms were showing some wear and tear, so do ask for a recently refurbished option if possible as, on inspection, they were far superior. Might I add that the staff at the Shibuya Granbell, while nice enough, are fairly, er, relaxed, which could be seen as a negative or a bonus depending on the type of traveller you are. The Granbell Hotels are good value for money in a city renowned for supremely expensive hotels with very small rooms!

HOTEL ALTERNATIVES

Ryokan (traditional inns)
The Ryokan Collection
ryokancollection.com/eng/
Although Kyoto is more closely affiliated with quality ryokan (traditional inns), there are still a few options in Tokyo and nearby village areas too. High-end ryokans are expensive, but an elaborate breakfast and Kaiseki-style Japanese dinner are often included as part of the package—sometimes they are additional.

Many people consider an exclusive ryokan stay a special treat and only spend a night or two— enjoying the onsen (natural spring bath) if they have one, sleeping on futon beds on the tatami floor, and dining on beautifully presented, delicious meals in their room served by graceful, kimono-clad hosts. However, there are some

more reasonably priced options available where the dining style and rooms are more casual, which makes a longer stay possible. It is definitely an experience worth having at least once.

Word of mouth from a friend is the best way to find the right ryokan for you, as it tends to be a more personal experience than a hotel stay. Failing that, visit the Japan Hotel and Ryokan Association for a list of quality establishments, or the Ryokan Collection for more luxury ryokan on the Tokyo outskirts.

Japan Hotel and Ryokan Association
ryokan.or.jp/english/

Apartment stays
tokyustay.co.jp/e/
The Tokyu Stay group of apartment-style hotels offers larger floor plans than many other hotels, with the added benefit of in-room kitchenettes with laundry facilities. They have fifteen venues dotted throughout the city and are clean and well serviced. With decent-sized desks in each room, free Wi-Fi and helpful, efficient front-desk staff, Tokyu Stay are a good option for business travellers or those on a longer visit.

Airbnb
airbnb.com
Due to the recent surge in tourism to Japan, Airbnb has really kicked off and become a popular and affordable Tokyo option—sometimes with a lot more space offered than hotel rooms. And, of course, it is a nice way to get to know local neighbourhoods where things are often a little more laid back than in the central city zone. Read between the lines with online reviews and recommendations, and make sure you choose a place close to public transport and amenities, such as convenience stores, supermarkets, pharmacies and so on. I like to look for places with a few local cafés or small restaurants too. Personally, when I travel alone I prefer to stay in hotels, as they are set up with emergency plans for things like earthquakes or fire—if you're nervous about such events, I'd save your Airbnb stay until you're with a travel buddy.

RESTAURANTS

Many casual dining suggestions are dotted through the walks in this guide for your convenience, but here are some of my fancier favourites—worth getting frocked up for!

❶ Shirosaka, Akasaka

tabelog.com/en/tokyo/A1308/A130801/13175154/

The superb, reasonably priced, set-course menu of kappo- (counter-) style restaurant Shirosaka showcases the creativity of Chef Ii, whose style is fresh and captivating while remaining deeply rooted in elegant tradition. Though the chef is certainly accomplished, he is considerably relaxed and friendly, and with a solid command of the English language, having worked overseas, he's happy to explain each cracking dish. The staff offer the warmest of welcomes and impeccable service. At Shirosaka it's easy for a foreigner to enjoy the kind of Japanese food to which they might not have access otherwise, and with a total of fifteen seats you'd better book … now!

❷ Two Rooms, Aoyama

tworooms.jp/en/

Respected Australian Chef Mathew Crabbe ensures the 'American Grill'-influenced menu is perfectly executed, from the crab cakes to roast chicken and teppan-grilled local pork. Simple dishes, done really well with just a smattering of traditional Japanese aromatics are a great way to introduce local flavours and ingredients to uninitiated palates. An outdoor terrace with a Manhattan-esque view of Tokyo calls for sipping one of their excellent shiso mojitos! Their Mont Blanc is a top-notch rendition—this dessert, even in its most simple forms, enjoys cult status all over Japan.

❸ Jimbocho Den, Jimbocho

http://www.jimbochoden.com/en/about.html

This is one of *the* most interesting and fun restaurant experiences in Tokyo. What makes Den most intriguing is that each spectacular offering from cheeky young chef Zaiyu Hasegawa possesses the kind of magic emotional element one might only expect from a much older, experienced and seriously learned chef. Hasegawa san appears to have been born with an inherently deep, almost spiritual

understanding of the truest Japanese cuisine—however, his youthful sense of humour and interpretive culinary dance style elevate things to a whole new level.

The hospitality is warm and seemingly casual—but faultless. The usual hushed tones of a Japanese restaurant serving food of this level are interspersed with laughter and groans of appreciation. All the seemingly mismatched facets of Jimbocho Den combine to form a wonderfully infectious dining experience—you crave to return even before you've finished your meal. Their two signature dishes give a good indication of what to expect on the menu: a starter monaka—usually a wafer casing for sweet bean confectionery, sandwiched with, for example, foie gras, dried persimmon and smoked daikon pickle; and their Dentucky Fried Chicken—perhaps filled with shiso, sesame and umeboshi seasoned rice, which comes in a takeaway box. It's more than finger-lickin' good. Just go. Some English spoken.

❹ Yakitori Seo, Maranouchi

thetokyostationhotel.jp/restaurants-bars/japanese.htm

Most hotel restaurants tend to leave me cold, but Yakitori Seo, underneath the beautiful Tokyo Station Hotel, is the real deal despite its relatively fancy setting. Perfectly grilled chicken and all of its parts, from fatty, delicious bonjiri (tail) to slim, full-flavoured seri (neck) can be ordered by the stick or as a course menu, with accompaniments such as chicken sashimi, pickles, grilled rice balls and a savoury chicken broth. The service is friendly and not as intimidating as it might be to venture to an under-track yakitori shack on your own. They won't scowl at you if you only order breast and thigh! Vegetarians take note—there are seasonal non-chicken sticks too! English menu available.

❺ Takazawa, Akasaka

http://www.takazawa-y.co.jp/en/

This tiny, upmarket restaurant run by a sophisticated husband and wife team is tucked away behind a quiet door in a sometimes rowdy food and bar district. You'd never stumble across it in a fit. I've been fortunate enough to have eaten here on several occasions over a ten-year period, and witnessed the highly creative and technically perfect food, and the restaurant's profile, blossom and boom. Much in the same way as each course in a traditional kaiseki meal is an ode to the season or a certain celebration, each

6

modern dish at Takazawa has a story behind it. Once explained (in perfect English), this makes the already visually pleasing food and marriage of flavours and textures even more impressive. It's hard to get into these days so do book well in advance. Sip a pre-dinner drink at their new bar around the corner—it also serves glamorous 'snacks' from the restaurant if you only have time or budget for a small taste of the master's cuisine.

❻ Narisawa, Aoyama
http://www.narisawa-yoshihiro.com/
One of Tokyo's most internationally famous contemporary restaurants promises diners the kind of performance you'd expect in a grand, albeit cutting-edge, theatre. You need to dedicate at least four hours to this feasting extravaganza and may in fact walk away shell-shocked by an almost over-abundance of beauty, drama

and pizzazz. Set in a simply appointed, spacious room with views into the kitchen to witness Chef Narisawa's magic, it will make you feel pampered from the moment you are seated and giddy with excitement from start to finish. From the bread that rises and cooks in a stone pot at your table to the small-batch, hard-to-find sake and freakish list of French wines, through the Okinawan sea snake soup (snake presented on request) and lobster tail with pretty petals or squid with 'smoking' ash dressing, all the way to the post-double-dessert trolley laden with petits fours that are displayed as though they've grown naturally in a forest setting—there's never a dull moment in Narisawa's playground. (Yes, they bring you two desserts *before* they roll out the trolley!) An 'only in Tokyo' experience.

Tempura Motoyoshi

motoyoshi-1120.com/category01/index02.html

A Zen-like tempura experience. Sit at the counter as each morsel of premium ingredient is cooked individually in front of you. The base ingredient is the hero. The batter, although so perfectly light and fragile, without a hint of residual oil, is almost inconsequential, which is what makes it so amazing. Every tempura chef has their own coating style. I often prefer the more robust, full-flavoured batter common in a casual tempura joint like **Tempura Takenawa** (p216), but this is from 'another mother'. It's one of those quiet, appreciative, contemplative Japanese dining experiences. You'll start with sashimi before working your way through seasonal land and mountain vegetables and fruits of the sea. The oil is changed halfway—even though there are less than ten people dining at any time. As is tradition, the meal ends with rice, pickles and soup, but here the rice component is in the form of a petite donburi (rice bowl) topped with seasonal kakiage (tempura fritter) and thickened dashi sauce, and the pickles are ginger—but not as you know it. The lovely, humble chef and his staff make you feel like part of the Motoyoshi family. A little English spoken.

❽ Alchemiste, Shirogane

alchimiste.jp/#chef

Having worked in some of France's most esteemed and cutting-edge restaurants, quiet but quirky Chef Yamamoto and his gorgeous, smart partner who works the floor serve up what they describe as 'popular gastronomy'—a contemporary French/Japanese menu. The dishes gradually escalate in creativity and intensity throughout the meal, like the stages of a flower blooming. The chef is a fan of murasaki (the colour purple) and you won't be able to miss his influence in the décor! The service is friendly and English is spoken.

❾ Jumbo Yakiniku, Shirogane

kuroge-wagyu.com/js/top_e.html

A firm favourite among Tokyoites, this upmarket grill-your-own-wagyu joint books out months in advance. Jumbo serves a selection of fine and curious cuts, and excellent kim chee. The service is fast and efficient, and they'll have turned your table over before you've paid, but the pace is what keeps up fun levels, the frosty beers a-coming and the folk returning. You'll reek of garlic for days, but that's all part of the enjoyment! Some English spoken.

7

7

8

8

BARS

Azabu Juban: Bar Gen Yamamoto
genyamamoto.jp/bar_tokyo/English.html
This is the bar you go to when you don't want to go to a bar. Almost in silence, the bartender–proprietor Gen Yamamoto, who once resided, shook and stirred in NYC, hand-juices, crushes, squeezes and pulps the most intensely perfumed and pure-flavoured fruits, vegetables and legumes into bases for his unique and utterly sublime cocktails. He mixes the fresh juices or extractions with fine and rare sake, shochu and spirits, balancing flavours in a way only a master could achieve— before transporting them across the counter to one of eight possible patrons. In the words of one of my favourite Tokyo people: 'I die.'

Shibuya: Red Bar (aka chandelier bar) (p47)
https://www.facebook.com/RED-BAR-980694541941323/

Ebisu: Bar Martha, Cavo, and Pile Cafe (p125–26)
martha-records.com/martha/, cavowinebar.jp/,
renovationplanning.co.jp/portfolio_page/pile-cafe-ebisu

Koenji: Sub Rosa (p160)
https://facebook.com/SUB-ROSA-161654607364375/

Asakusa: Bar Six (p209)

Kuramae: Nui (p224) **backpackersjapan.co.jp/nui_en/**

Kanda: N331 and The Hitachino Brewing Lab (p239)
n3331.com/, hitachino.cc/brewing-lab/

Yanesen: Sankenma (p257) **taireki.com/sankenma/**

The earthy izakaya/bars of Tokyo's Yokocho (alleys) and Gado-shita (beneath the girders): Nonbei Yokocho, including Red Bar, Shibuya (p47); Ebisu Yokocho, Ebisu (p126); Harmonica Yokocho, Kichijoji (p148); Koenji gado-shita, Koenji (p162) **nonbei.tokyo, ebisu-yokocho.com/top.html**

See the Hotel & Restaurant sections for more recommended bars.

MUSEUMS & GALLERIES

Nezu Museum, Aoyama (p71)
www.nezu-muse.or.jp/en/index.html

The National Art Centre, Roppongi (p71) www.nact.jp/english/

Mingei-kan, Meguro—folkcraft museum (p90)
www.mingeikan.or.jp/

Kyu Asakura House, Daikanyama (p103)
city.shibuya.tokyo.jp/est/asakura.html

Hara Museum Of Contemporary Art, Shinagawa (p121)
www.haramuseum.or.jp/generalTop.html

Tokyo Metropolitan Museum of Photography, Ebisu (p125)
syabi.com/english.php

Museum of Yebisu Beer, Ebisu (p125)
sapporoholdings.jp/english/guide/yebisu/

Ghibli Museum, Mitaka (p136) ghibli-museum.jp/

AMUSE museum, Asakusa (p208) amusemuseum.com/english/

Asakura Choso, Yanaka—sculpture museum (p250)
taitocity.net/taito/asakura/english/index.html

HAGISO, Yanaka (p253) hagiso.jp/

Scai the Bathhouse, Yanaka (p258) scaithebathhouse.com/en/

Tokyo National Museum, Ueno (p264) tnm.jp/

**Miraikan, Odaiba Island—national museum of emerging
science and innovation** *(right)* www.miraikan.jst.go.jp/en/

MARKETS

There is a host of regular and irregular farmers' markets, flea markets and antique markets dotted around the city. Keep your eyes and ears peeled for them, as they promise certain treasures. Here's a starter list.

HANDICRAFTS MARKETS

Tezukuri Ichi, Ikebukuro
kishimojin.jp/map/index.html (location)
tezukuriichi.com/entry.html#07 (schedule)
Held in the Kishimojin temple grounds, this market is a little tricky to locate, but it's absolutely worth seeking out for an array of original, well-made, handcrafted goods. Held on third Sunday of the month.

Akaji Jinja, Kagurazaka (p188)
akagimarche.blogspot.jp/

FARMERS' MARKETS

UNU Farmers Market, Shibuya (p56)
ourworld.unu.edu/en/farmers-market-comes-to-the-un

Earth Day Market, various
earthdaymarket.com/
Popular and mostly organic, this market has a holistic, environmentally friendly, universally bonding aim. Offers some non-food goods, such as ceramics and jewellery, too.

FLEA MARKETS

Yoyogi Park Flea Market, Shibuya (p35) yoyogipark.info/

Tokyo Recycle, various trx.jp/
Shinjuku Central Park Flea Market, Shinjuku

http://www.jinsei-geki.com/FormMail/kaijyou-sinjyuku.html
Good for vintage.

Yasakuni Shrine Flea Market, Chiyoda
homepage3.nifty.com/kankyo-1997/index.htm

ANTIQUE MARKETS

Oedo Antique Market in Yoyogi Park, Shibuya (p35)
yoyogipark.info/2015/antique-market-2016/

Heiwajima, Shinkjuku
kottouichi.com/heiwajima/ENGLISH.html

TSUKIJI FISH MARKET, CHUO
tsukiji-market.or.jp/tukiji_e.htm
Tokyo's famous fish market has always been a great place to witness a rollicking, raw side of Tokyo life, and more seafood species than you could dream up. There are some early morning tours of the market but you can go on your own—just be respectful, stay out of the way of fast-moving vehicles, and wear a pair of shoes you don't care that much for. It's all over by about 9 am-ish, so go early, and then buy yourself a sushi breakfast at the stalls outside the northwest mouth of the market. As I write, the market is on the move to larger, more modern premises and visiting rights may change. Until then, go for it. **Jogai Shijo**, the outer market right next door, is better set up for visitors, and makes a great visual introduction to local fresh and preserved ingredients—meat, vegetables, pickles and dried goods.

OTHER THINGS I LIKE TO DO

PEOPLE-WATCHING

A 10-minute walk northwest of gritty Tsukiji fish market and you are in a whole new world—the uber-ritzy shopping area of **Ginza**. The main strip of Chuo Dori is closed on weekends to everything but human (and dog) traffic. It's a great time to stroll and window-shop, gazing at glamorous high-end boutique displays. Think diamonds, pearls, couture, and shoes that look like they should never meet feet. However, the main attraction for me is watching the movement, style and interactions of the people on the street, who travel at a far more carefree pace than on the weekdays. **ginza.jp/en/**

MORE FOOD

One of my favourite food-related things to do in Japan is visit the depachika—underground food halls—in Tokyo. I particularly like **Isetan** in Shinjuku, **Daimaru** (next to Tokyo Station), **Tobu** in Ikebukuro, **Takashimaya** in Nihonbashi and **Ginza's Mitsukoshi** for both inspiration and picnics, whether in a park or hotel room! If you're visiting in cherry-blossom season or autumn, snaffle a spot under a tree with some depachika snacks and drink in your surrounds.

Visit the under-track 'gaado-shita' (under the girders) yakitori-ya, ramen-ya and izakaya at Yurakucho Station and the tiny ramshackle izakaya of omoide yokocho (memory lane) at Shinjuku Station—the food isn't necessarily great, but you go for the atmosphere, the beer and sake, the local characters and superb photo opportunities! **shinjuku-omoide.com/**

If you have a hankering for ramen, visit the Tokyo Station **Ramen Street** for eight competing top ramen shops. Go really early or be prepared to queue for some time.
tokyoeki-1bangai.co.jp/street/ramen
tokyoeki-1bangai.co.jp/pdf/floorMap_foreign.pdf

Japanese sweets: Stop for matcha (whisked green tea) and wagashi (traditional tea sweets) at **Toraya, Ginza**. **toraya-group.co.jp/**

The **Shin Marunouchi Building** near Tokyo Station is home to one of the fanciest food halls ever! **http://www.marunouchi.com/e/shop?type=top**

ROOFTOP BARS

I'm not averse to a Tokyo rooftop bar, either in hotels or on the top of some restaurants or office buildings. Many of them go under the radar so you need to keep an eye out. They often have incredible views and, in summer, rooftop beer gardens can provide cool relief (if only mentally). My advice: look up. If you can see lights and glowing lanterns on top of a building, chances are …

MORE SHOPPING

Check out the **Kitte** building for seven floors of fabulous shopping, including a whole floor of gorgeous Japanese homewares and décor. **https://jptower-kitte.jp/en/**

MORE ARCHITECTURE

There's so much to love about Tokyo's architecture, and every day brings fascinating new additions. Toranamon Hills is one of my favourites; you won't be disappointed. Great range of eateries too. **http://toranomonhills.com/en/**

FURTHER AFIELD

If you're planning an extended stay in Tokyo you may well be drawn to a short break in a nearby town, away from the sometimes blinding lights of the big city.

MOUNT FUJI AND HAKONE

The main islands of Japan are extremely mountainous and volcanic, and one of the reasons why the liveable areas are so densely populated. By far the most impressive and important of all Japan's mountains is the sacred and iconic Fuji san.
fujisan-climb.jp/en/

You might be yet to visit Japan, but you could probably pick the mountain's impressive cone shape out in a line-up. There is much folklore surrounding **Mount Fuji**, and the Japanese feel strongly connected to its energy—a pilgrimage at least part way up is on the bucket list for most of the population.

Many locals and foreign sporty types hike a portion of the 3776-metre-high mount during the warmer months. In winter, it's difficult to make it past a certain point due to heavy snow. Located just 100 kilometres southwest of Tokyo, and easily seen on a clear day from taller buildings in the city, it's a popular day trip for tourists. However, organised full-day bus tours usually take you as far as the fifth station up the mountain—weather permitting. They only stop for a few minutes for a photo opportunity before heading back down to the **Hakone area** at the base of the mountain, where you inevitably take a short boat ride on **Lake Ashi**. Perhaps the tour will return via a cable-car ride above the sulphurous bubbling mud ponds of volcanic **Owakudani valley** on your way back to Tokyo. It is a whirlwind ticking-boxes kind of day, and great if you're time poor. For a truer appreciation of the region, stay in the nearby hot springs resort area of **Hakone**—just over an hour by train southwest of Tokyo. hakonenavi.jp/english/traffic/

Stay in a traditional inn—*see* ryokan accommodation p275. If you choose wisely, you'll have a view of Mount Fuji. Take some time to explore the quaint local village, shopping for handicrafts, and then hop on a boat ride around Lake Ashi at your leisure. You may also wish to visit the popular **open-air museum**. hakone-oam.or.jp/

If you wish to be on the mountain itself, there are a couple of access options using buses or trains to the **Fuji Five Lakes** area at the base of the mountain. Your accommodation front desk or the local tourist office will be able to assist you. jnto.go.jp/eng/location/spot/tic/14022660.html

Hakone map link
hakonenavi.jp/english/traffic/rout_map/pdf/hakone_map.pdf

KAMAKURA

Home to one of Japan's famous Daibutsu (giant Buddha statues) is the charming coastal town of Kamakura, an easy 50–60-minute trip south, via train from Tokyo Station.
city.kamakura.kanagawa.jp/kamakura-kankou/en/

As one of the de facto ancient capitals of Japan, Kamakura has a special vibe and culture of its own. It's rich with stunning temples and shrines, as well as a relaxed beachside culture should you decide to linger for a couple of nights. **Kamakura village** itself is small enough to explore in a day by foot, but worthy of a couple of days if you have time on your side. Although the sites suggested below are on the usual tourist routes, they are definitely highlights and worth visiting. However, there are many quieter, more peaceful options.

For a day trip, visit **Kotokuin Temple** to meet the handsome Daibutsu (giant Buddha statues), and **Hasedera Temple** for a stroll through the

pretty garden up to a viewing platform over **Kamakura Bay**.
kotoku-in.jp/en/about/about.html
hasedera.jp/en/about/
The main drag around Kamakura Station has plenty of small shops
and restaurants, and while a little touristy, it is still fun to wander.
To the north of the village is the small but well-curated **Museum
of Modern Art**.
www.moma.pref.kanagawa.jp/en/index.html

KAWAGOE

koedo.or.jp/foreign/english/
Just half an hour by express train north of Ikebukuro, but feeling
much further away, is quaint Kawagoe. This old castle town was
once an important merchant city ruled by the Kawagoe clan. While

it's admittedly rather touristy in parts, Kawagoe is home to some of the most stunning and best-preserved architecture in the area, particularly in the old kurazukuri (storehouse) zone and surrounds. Photographically, it's a dream, with a number of buildings left standing from each of the Edo, Meiji, Taisha and Showa periods (1603–1989), making it also an interesting visit for history buffs.

There's a loop bus from the station for easy access to points of interest, and the town proudly spruiks its own craft beer, Coedo— now gaining traction internationally.

Kawagoe is famous for local sweets. Kashiya Yokocho (Penny Lane) is an alleyway dedicated to its impressive collection—some handmade with natural ingredients, some the gravel of Japanese childhood nostalgia. Watching visiting kids whooping it up is half the fun. Local crafts make for good souvenirs, and shops are plentiful. ●

GLOSSARY

chawan mushi: steamed savoury custard, usually cooked and served in a Japanese teacup called a chawan.

chiyogami: a word used to describe Edo-period-inspired graphic, repetitive designs printed on paper (commonly used for decorative crafts and origami). Originally they were printed by hand-carved woodblock.

chuuhai: an alcoholic beverage containing shochu (a strong distilled liquor commonly made from sweet potato, rice, grains or brown sugar) mixed with fresh fruit juice or flavoured syrup and soda water.

conbini: (also konbini) convenience store

cosplayers: people who dress in anime and manga (Japanese animation and comic) character-inspired costumes. They parade or perform in public, taking on a particular character's personality. It is often taken quite seriously by both the cosplayer and their audience.

dashi: the cornerstone broth of Japanese cuisine, made from kombu (kelp seaweed) and katsuobushi (dried, fermented and smoked fish— often skipjack or bonito tuna) and sometimes other dried fish species.

depachika: basement food hall in department stores

doki-ya: copper shop

donburi: individual, often largish, deep bowls of hot rice topped with one of a large variety of flavourful toppings. The word is commonly shortened to 'don' when proceeded by the topping name. For example, the popular oyako donburi (a mix of chicken, onions and egg simmered in a sweetened soy broth over rice) becomes okayo-don. Tonkatsu-don is rice topped with sliced fried pork (tonkatsu), ikura-don is topped with salmon roe (ikura), ten-don is topped with tempura and on it goes …

dori: street

ebi furai: deep-fried crumbed prawns

ema: small wooden plaques sold in Shinto shrines upon one side of which worshippers write their prayers or wishes. They are left tied in the shrine grounds for the gods or spirits to receive them. Originally horses (uma) were donated to shrines in the hope of good fortune in business, happiness, relationships, health and so on. When that became less practical, the rectangular-ish wooden tablets or 'ema' (the word for a drawn horse) were offered instead—handmade and decorated with the painting of a horse on one side. These days ema are commonly decorated with something symbolic of the shrine itself, the season or the year, or the specific year's zodiac animal.

honten: main shop

ikebana: traditional Japanese flower arrangement

izakaya: traditionally a place to drink sake (originally at sake shops), where small snacks were served as a gesture of hospitality. These days izakaya refers to casual eating and drinking establishments that sell a variety of alcohol and small plates of food for sharing. Some are cheap and cheerful with alcohol the main event and are popular with students and young travellers; others offer better food and a variety of high-quality sake.

kagura: literally translating as 'entertainment for the gods', refers most commonly to dance or music with roots in Shintoism.

Kaiseki cuisine: in simple terms, a traditional, high-end Japanese cuisine form, with humble roots in the Buddhist tea ceremony. Commonly around twelve small courses are exquisitely presented on beautiful tableware—often by kimono-clad waitresses. Each dish tells a story of the season, a celebration or a significant event.

kani: crab

katsu-sando: katsu (Japanese for 'cutlet') are flattish pieces of crumbed and deep-fried pork, chicken or beef sandwiched between two slices of white bread, often with a special sweetly spiced sauce made specifically for katsu and/or hot mustard. Modern versions may include shredded lettuce and Japanese mayonnaise.

kawaii: cute

kim chee: Korean pickles

kinako: roasted soy bean flour

kissaten: western-style tea and coffee shops first introduced to Japan during the Meiji era (1868–1912). The 1950s and 1960s boasted the peak of their popularity. Sadly, many have disappeared, replaced by contemporary coffee shops and chain-store cafés. Those kissaten left standing are often terrifically atmospheric and offer a charming 'only in Japan' experience—even through the cloud of salaryman-produced cigarette smoke.

koban: small police stations dotted throughout Japanese neighbourhoods.

machiya: translating as 'town shops' or 'town houses', machiya are handsome, traditional wooden buildings of one to three storeys where merchants or craftspeople both lived and traded from as early as the Heian period (794–1185). The shop was situated at the front at ground level, with the dwelling behind or above. In centuries past, many machiya burned down either accidentally or purposely. In more recent times, they were destroyed in the name of 'progress'. Most remaining machiya are between 100 and 200 years old. There is now a movement to preserve them, particularly in Kyoto. They are being lovingly restored as shops, homes and accommodation.

matsuri: festival

minchi katsu: a type of minced beef and potato cake (or cutlet) either shallow- or deep-fried until golden.

monozukuri: rather humbly translating as 'making things'. The term commonly refers to quality handmade or crafted items made with great care, attention and heart.

mottainai: loosely translates as 'a regretfulness regarding waste', a term used when wishing for self or others to be more conscious of using or re-using in an effort to avoid waste.

nabe: the shortened version of donabe, which is the word used for both the vessel in which simmered/hotpot dishes are made, and the particular food made in it. Much like we say we are eating 'casserole'—named for the dish in which it is made and often served.

obaachan: grandmother/s

obi: kimono sash

oden: a full-flavoured winter hotpot dish where a variety of ingredients such as fishcakes, tofu in different forms, daikon, meatballs and whole eggs are simmered in a dashi-based broth. There are many regional variations, some containing miso, others soy. Richer versions contain slowly simmered gelatinous meats, such as beef shin and pig trotters.

okonomiyaki: a type of 'as you like it' savoury pancake containing shredded cabbage, ground yam and a mix of other vegetables, meats (often pork or bacon), sometimes seafood of your choice and sometimes noodles. The mixture is cooked on a hot, flat grill plate, often in front of you at the table, to a desired texture—some more crisp, others a little tender. Okonomiyaki are commonly topped with a specially made thick, dark, sweetish sauce similar to worcestershire sauce, Japanese mayonnaise, katsuobushi and/or nori flakes, and sometimes pickles or sliced spring onions. Some are topped with eggs or more elaborate modern westernised sauces.

omu-rice: omelette wrapped around seasoned rice

omukuji: a 'fortune' written on paper, which can be purchased at temples and shrines.

onsen: natural hot-spring bath

otaku: loosely translating as 'someone who is completely obsessed with a specific topic—sometimes to the point of being unhealthy'. While it originated as a negative term, it is now sometimes used in the way you might call someone a 'nerd'— socially awkward perhaps, but full of knowledge about something in particular.

oyatsu pan: a snack-sized, soft fluffy bread (often in flattish rounds) with sweet and savoury fillings or toppings.

rosu katsu: sliced sirloin of pork (sometimes beef), crumbed and deep-fried—popular at tonkatsu restaurants as it contains a higher level of flavoursome fat than hire (filet) katsu.

ryokan: traditional inn

ryotei: traditional restaurants featuring exquisite Kaiseki cuisine

sakura: cherry blossom

sakura mochi: cherry-blossom-flavoured rice and bean sweets

salaryman: dark-suited, white-collar office workers

senbei: rice crackers

shinkansen: bullet train

shiso: an aromatic Japanese summer herb with a large green leaves

shitamachi: downtown, a direct translation of 'shita' (down) and 'machi' (town). It has a slightly different meaning from the English use of 'downtown'. In Japan, these are the poorer areas of town where the 'common' folk lived, as opposed to the wealthy and the aristocracy— feudal lords, samurai and so on. We are talking way back in the Edo period (1603–1867).

shochu: a distilled Japanese liquor commonly made from sweet potato, brown sugar, barley, buckwheat or rice. It contains 25–45 per cent alcohol and can pack a punch! The flavour is more pronounced and often more robust than sake, which is a brewed rice liquor.

shogun: the top military commander in feudal Japan. The last shogun died in 1913.

shoji: sliding screen-like walls or doors made of lightweight wood or bamboo lattice and washi (translucent paper). Used to separate rooms in traditional Japanese houses.

shotengai: shopping strip, sometimes covered arcades and sometimes open-air. Often terribly old-fashioned!

stupa board: in Buddhist architecture a 'stupa' is a monument, sometimes containing relics or items of religious significance. In Japan, a 'stupa board' is a stone tablet that simply gives the name of a deceased person, the date and the name of the person who submitted the board to a temple graveyard as part of the funeral ritual.

taiyaki: fish-shaped pancakes, most commonly filled with sweet red bean paste and sometimes cream or custard cream in a variety of flavours.

takoyaki: a popular street food, regularly described as 'octopus balls'. These ball-shaped 'popovers', made from a batter containing chopped octopus and pickled ginger, are cooked in a special takoyaki grill pan and usually slathered with an okonomiyaki-style sauce, Japanese mayonnaise and nori flakes or chopped spring onion.

tatami: uniform rectangular flooring mats used in traditional Japanese-style rooms. Compacted rice straw or cheaper, more commercial products are topped with woven rush straw, the edges of which are bound with brocade or plain cloth. Traditional rooms have always been measured by the number of tatami they contain.

tezukuri: handmade

tonkatsu: deep-fried, crumbed or breaded pork cutlet—commonly a thick slice of sirloin or pieces of fillet.

torii: Shinto shrine gates found at the entrance or within the shrine itself, marking the transition into the sacred space. Traditionally torii are made from wood and either left natural or painted vermilion.

tsukudani: foodstuffs preserved by cooking slowly in a soy and mirin base. Common ingredients are kombu, dried vegetables, such as shiitake mushrooms, and small quantities of certain fish or meat. Tiny amounts of the salty preserve are eaten as a condiment or a snack with drinks.

tsurushi shuto: authentic deer leather

wa-mono: traditional Japanese goods

wagashi: traditional Japanese confectionery

washi: handmade paper, predominantly from the bark fibres of the paper mulberry tree. Can also be made from other products, such as bamboo, rice and hemp. Washi is usually stronger than paper made from wood and can be thickly textured, natural or smooth and opaque. Common in Japanese arts and crafts.

yakiniku: translating directly as 'grilled meat', but in reality it's so much more: various cuts of meat and offal, predominantly beef or pork, served with marinades and sauces heavily influenced by Korean cuisine. It's popular to cook your own yakiniku on a table-top grill.

yakisoba: a flavoursome, stir-fried noodle dish containing meat, such as pork, beef, chicken, bacon or seafood, a variety of vegetables and yakisoba sauce—another derivative of the worcestershire-style sauces so popular in Japan. Although the name is confusing, the dish is not made with soba noodles, which are too fragile to flip around, but a wheat noodle similar to, but thicker than, ramen noodles.

yakitori: Literally translating as 'grilled chicken', yakitori usually refers to small pieces of chicken flesh, meatballs, skin or innards threaded onto short bamboo skewers and grilled to perfection—either simply with salt, or 'tare' a slightly sweet soy, mirin and chicken-stock glaze.

yukata: lightweight summer kimono, usually made from cotton or synthetic.

yuzu: Japanese citrus used for its stunningly aromatic rind and juice. Used regularly in winter when it's in season.

zaka: slope

zakka: miscellaneous décor items and knick-knacks

WEBSITES

HARAJUKU & SHIBUYA

1   **Meiji Jingu (shrine):** meijijingu.or.jp/english/index.html
2   **Yoyogi Koen (park):** tokyo-park.or.jp/park/format/index039.html
3   **Takeshita Street:** takeshita-street.com/index.html
4   **Cat Street**
5   **Omotesando Hills:** omotesandohills.com/english/
6   **Golden Brown:** goldenbrown.info/
7   **Oriental Bazaar:** orientalbazaar.co.jp/en/
8   **Gyre building:** gyre-omotesando.com/
9   **MoMA store:** momastore.jp/momastore/
10 **Magnolia Bakery:** magnoliabakery.com/locations/japan-jingumae-shibuya-ku/
11 **Kiddy Land:** kiddyland.co.jp/en/
12 **Quico:** quico.jp/
13 **The Roastery by Nozy Coffee:** tysons.jp/roastery/
14 **Scrapbook (Jeanasis):** scrapbook-jeanasis.com/
15 **C-Plus Head Wares:** www.c-plus.jp/
16 **Pink Dragon:** pinkdragon.co.jp/

17 **BIC Camera Store:** biccamera.co.jp/shoplist/shop-008.html
18 **Five-way crossing**
19 **Nonbei Yokocho:** nonbei.tokyo
20 **Red Bar**
21 **Shibuya 109:** jreast.co.jp/e/stations/e808.html
22 **Hikarie:** hikarie.jp/en/

AOYAMA

1   **Farmers' market at the United Nations University (UNU):** ourworld.unu.edu/en/farmers-market-comes-to-the-un
2   **Pierre Hermé:** pierreherme.co.jp/aoyama.html
3   **Found Muji:** muji.net/foundmuji/
4   **Momotaro Jeans:** momotarojeans.net/site/
5   **Two Rooms:** tworooms.jp/
6   **OPA gallery shop:** opagallery.net/
7   **Bread and Espresso:** bread-espresso.jp/
8   **Lattest Omotesando Espresso Bar:** lattest.jp/
9   **Mr. FARMER:** eat-walk.com/mf/index.html
10 **Maisen:** mai-sen.com/ (*see* English page)

11 **Gallery Kawano:**
gallery-kawano.com/

12 **nest Robe:** nestrobe.com/

13 **Brown Rice Canteen:** www.
nealsyard.co.jp/brownrice/

14 **Shito Hisayo:**
www.shito-hisayo.jp/index.
html

15 **Daimonji:** www.daimonji.biz/

16 **APC:**
apc.fr/wwuk/store-finder/

17 **Shoyeido:**
www.shoyeido.co.jp/

18 **Lisn:** www.lisn.co.jp/

19 **Bloom & Branch:**
bloom-branch.jp/

20 **Tsutaya:** profile.ameba.jp/
tsutayashouten/

21 **Madu:** hakka-online.jp/
brand/madu/?link=HD_
MAU01

22 **Higashiya:** higashiya.com/

23 **Plain People:** one-be-one.com/

24 **Nezu Museum:** www.nezu-
muse.or.jp/en

25 **The National Art Centre:**
nact.jp/english/

26 **Souvenir from Tokyo:**
www.souvenirfromtokyo.jp/

27 **Blue Bottle:** bluebottlecoffee.
com/cafes/aoyama

28 **Commune 246:**
commune246.com/

SHIMOKITAZAWA

1 **Ichibangai:**
shimokita1ban.com/

2 **Sencha:** sen-cha.com/

3 **Slick mist:** slickmist.com/

4 **Marble Sud:**
marble-sud.com/
about/#shimokitazawa

5 **Soffitto:**
melrose.co.jp/soffitto/

6 **Natural Laundry:**
naturallaundry.com/shop_
shimokita/

7 **Pinkertons:** rakuten.ne.jp/
gold/pinkerton/

8 **Ruelle:** barns-shop.com/

9 **Antique Life Jin:**
antiquelife-jin.com/

10 **Alaska vintage clothing:**
alaska-tokyo.jp/

11 **Flamingo:** tippirag.com/
shopsyo_flamingo#

12 **The Sun Goes Down:**
thesungoesdown.jp/

13 **Shimokitazawa Garage
Department:** k-toyo.jp/

14 **B-Side Label:**
bside-label.com/top1.html

15 **Bear Pond Espresso:**
bear-pond.com/

16 **N.Y. Cupcakes Cupcakery:**
cupcakes.jp/

17 **8 Jours:**
cafe8jour0.wix.com/8-jours

18 **Tenmaya Curry Pan:**
tabelog.com/en/tokyo/
A1318/A131802/13163101/

19 **Antiquaille:** antiquaille.jp/

20 **Suzunari:** honda-geki.com/
suzunari2.html

21 **Theater 711:**
honda-geki.com/711.html

22 **Suzunari Yokocho**

23 **Mingei-kan:** mingeikan.or.jp/

DAIKANYAMA & NAKA MEGURO

1. **TENOHA & Style:** tenoha.jp/
2. **Hollywood Ranch Market:** hrm.co.jp/hrm/
3. **Rawlife:** blog.rawlife-jp.com/
4. **Ivy Place:** tysons.jp/ivyplace/
5. **Daikanyama T-site:** tsite.jp/daikanyama/
6. **Hillside Terrace:** hillsideterrace.com/index2.html
7. **Makié Home:** makiehome.com/shop
8. **Greeniche:** www.greeniche.jp/
9. **Kyu Asakura House:** city.shibuya.tokyo.jp/est/asakura.html
10. **Life's:** lifes-203.com/shop.html
11. **Hokodo Bijutsu:** hookodo.co.jp/
12. **Evisu the Tokyo:** evisu.jp/
13. **H:** jumpinjapflash.com/h/shop/
14. **Have a Good Time:** have-a-goodtime.com/
15. **Brick & Mortar:** brickandmortar.jp/
16. **Snobbish babies:** www.asknowas.com/dewan/stores_nakameguro.html
17. **bulle de savon:** ambidex.co.jp/bulle_de_savon/index.php
18. **Red Clover:** www.red-clover.jp/
19. **Carlife:** iqon.jp/store/nakameguro/7125/
20. **ACTS:** acts97.com/
21. **Hosu:** hosu.jp/
22. **Telepathy Route:** telepathyroute.com/
23. **Ouvrage Classe:** pal-blog.jp/brand/ouvrage/shop/nakameguro
24. **Jean Nassaus Hale o Pua:** jean-nassaus.co.jp/retail-store/
25. **Leah-K:** leah-k.jp/
26. **Kapuki:** kapuki.jp/
27. **Minamo:** mi-na-mo.jp/index.html

MEGURO

1. **Claska Hotel:** claska.com/
2. **Do:** claska.com/shop/index.html
3. **Fusion Interiors:** fusion-interiors.com/
4. **Otsu furniture:** demode-furniture.net/otsu/shop/
5. **Geographica:** geographica.jp/
6. **Catii Tokyo:** store.catii.jp/
7. **Pour Annick:** pourannick.com/
8. **Blackboard by karf:** karf.co.jp/blackboard/
9. **Brunch + one:** brunchone.com/brunch-one/
10. **Fake Furniture:** fakefurnituretokyo.com/
11. **Moody's:** moody-s.net/junks.html
12. **Sonechika:** sonechika.blog47.fc2.com/
13. **Silk:** demode-furniture.net/silk/shop/
14. **Lewis:** lewis-meguro.com/

15 karf: karf.co.jp/

16 Brunch + sc: brunchone.com/
brunch-works/

17 Chambre de nîmes brocante:
chambre.innocent.co.jp/

18 Junks: moody-s.net/junks.html

19 Gallery. S: gallery-s.jp/

20 Brunch + time: brunchone.
com/brunch-works/

21 brunch + works: brunchone.
com/brunch-works/

22 Point no. 39: p39-clowns.com/

23 Antoine Careme:
tabelog.com/en/tokyo/A1316/
A131601/13008284/

24 Boulangerie Jolly:
tabelog.com/en/tokyo/A1317/
A131701/13126480/

25 Kunima Coffee:
kunimacoffee.com/

26 Aburamen Park:

27 Neiro: neiro-r.com/

28 Gakugeidaigaku Station

29 Ebisu Station

**30 Hara Museum of
Contemporary Art:**
haramuseum.or.jp/
generalTop.html

EBISU

1 Yebisu Garden Place:
gardenplace.jp/

**2 Mitsukoshi Department
Store:** mitsukoshi.mistore.jp/
store/ebisu/index.html

**3 Tokyo Metropolitan
Museum of Photography:**
topmuseum.jp

4 Museum of Yebisu Beer:
sapporoholdings.jp/english/
guide/yebisu/

5 Cavo: facebook.com/
pages/cavo-wine-
bar/132489003488137

6 Pile Café:
renovationplanning.co.jp/
portfolio_page/pile-cafe-
ebisu

7 Ebisu Yokocho:
ebisu-yokocho.com/top.html

8 Bar Martha:
martha-records.com/
martha/

KICHIJOJI, KOENJI & NAKANO

KICHIJOJI

1 Rose Bakery:
rosebakery.jp/access/

2 Artre shopping mall:
atre.co.jp.e.ww.hp.transer.
com/store/kichijoji

3 Marui department store:
0101.co.jp/stores/guide/
store160.html

4 L'epicurien:
tabelog.com/en/tokyo/
A1320/A132001/13005891/

5 Inokashira Park:
kensetsu.metro.tokyo.jp/
seibuk/inokashira/

6 Inokashira Benzaiten:
inokashirabenzaiten.com/
english.htm

7 Ghibli Museum:
ghibli-museum.jp/

NAKANO

1 Sun Mall
2 Nakano Broadway: nbw.jp/index_e.html
3 Back to MONO: rakuten.co.jp/backtomono/index.html
4 MMTS: mmts-shop.jp/
5 Teketeke Izakaya: teke-teke.com/

KAGURAZAKA & KORAKUEN

1 Koishikawa Korakuen Garden: kensetsu.metro.tokyo.jp/kouen/kouennannai/park/english/koishikawa.pdf
2 Canal Café: canalcafe.jp/
3 Tsubaki-ya: per-fume.jp/
4 GOJUUBAN honten: 50ban-honten.jp
5 Makanai: e-makanai.com/
6 Zenkoku-ji: kagurazaka-bishamonten.com/
7 Le Bretagne: le-bretagne.com/e/
8 La Ronde d'Argile shop: la-ronde.com/
9 Isuzu: isuzu-wagashi.co.jp/
10 Baikatei: baikatei.co.jp/
11 Kimuraya: kimuraya-enet.co.jp/tizu/tizu.htm
12 Little Mermaid Bakery: littlemermaid.jp/index.html
13 Craftman Manou: http://shinjuku.mypl.net/kosodate_support/00000000320/14

14 La Terre: wing2014.jp/index.html
15 Enfukutera and enpukuji: enpuku-ji.jp/
16 Akagi Jinja (shrine): akagi-jinja.jp/
17 Akagi café: akagi-cafe.jp/
18 Bon Riviere: facebook.com/Bonriviere1998 and http://tabelog.com/en/tokyo/A1309/A130905/13118915/?rvwid=7238407
19 Le Kagu: lakagu.com/
20 KADO: kagurazaka-kado.com/

ASAKUSA & KAPPABASHI

1 Kaminarimon Gate: www.senso-ji.jp/
2 Asakusa Cultural Information Centre: gotokyo.org/en/kanko/taito/spot/s_983.html
3 Nakamise: http://asakusa-nakamise.jp/e-index.html
4 Kanzashiya Wargo: kanzashiya.com/
5 Kuriko-an: http://kurikoan.com/
6 Kineya: asakusa-nakamise.jp/shop-3/kineya/e-index.html
7 Kiryudo: ab.auone-net.jp/~kiryudo/asakusa.html
8 Haneda: http://hanayome.biz/wa/detail/haneda.html
9 Hozomon Gate
10 Sensooji: http://www.senso-ji.jp/about/index_e.html

11 **Tokyo Skytree:**
tokyo-skytree.jp/en
12 **Asakusa Shrine:**
http://www.asakusajinja.jp/
english/
13 **AMUSE Museum:**
www.amusemuseum.com/
14 **Bar Six**
15 **Marble:**
hanayome.biz/wa/detail/
marble2.html
16 **Hanayashiki:**
hanayashiki.net/e/
17 **Asakusa Dougin Douki:**
item.rakuten.
co.jp/hachimitu-
create/c/0000000190/
18 **Carbo:** carbo2010.com/
19 **Sekine Bakery:**
tabelog.com/en/tokyo/A1311/
A131102/13110040/
20 **Meugaya:**
asakusa.gr.jp/shop/
myogaya.html
21 **Kappabashi:** kappabashi.
or.jp/en/index.html.
22 **Nishiyama's:** shikki.jp/
23 **Kamata:** kap-kam.com/
index_english.html
24 **Maizuru:** maiduru.co.jp/
25 **Asakusa Maekawa
Tsurushi Shuto:**
maekawa-inden.co.jp/
26 **Asakusa Mori Gin:**
asakusamorigin.com/
27 **Tempura Takenawa:**
tabelog.com/en/tokyo/A1311/
A131102/13008619/
28 **The Gate Hotel:**
www.gate-hotel.jp/english/

**KURAMAE, OKACHIMACHI,
AKIHABARA & KANDA-
OCHANOMIZU**

1 **Koncent:** koncent.net/shop
2 **Nui:** backpackersjapan.co.jp/
nui_en/
3 **Cielo y Rio:** cieloyrio.com/
4 **New Old Stock by Otogi:**
otogi-designs.com/shop.html
5 **In-Kyo:** in-kyo.net/
6 **M+:** m-piu.com/
7 **Maito:** maitokomuro.com/
8 **REN:** ren-madeintokyo.com/
9 **CC4441:** cc4441.com/
10 **SYU-RO:** syuro.info/
11 **Okazu Yokocho:** jec.ac.jp/
work/website/w_03/data/
index.html
12 **Tsubamekobo:**
tsubamekobo.com/
13 **Taito Designers Village:**
designers-village.com/
14 **BRASS:**
brassblog.exblog.jp/i6/
15 **Carmine**
16 **Shin Okachimachi station**
17 **Ueno-Okachimachi station**
18 **Okachimachi station**
19 **2k540 Aki-Oka Artisan:**
jrtk.jp/2k540/
20 **The Nippon Department
Store:** nippon-dept.jp/store
21 **Hacoa:**
hacoa.com/index.html
22 **Studio Uamou:** uamou.com
23 **Nakazawa:**
nakazawa2k540.tokyo/
24 **Tokyo Noble:**
tokyo-noble.com/

25 **Chabara:** jrtk.jp/chabara/

26 **Maach e cute:**
maach-ecute.jp/

27 **The Hitachino Brewing Lab:**
hitachino.cc/brewing-lab/

28 **N331:** n3331.com/

29 **Fukumori:** fuku-mori.jp/
bakurocho/

30 **Ochanomizu Brick Mall:**
foursquare.com/v/%E3%83
%96%E3%83%AA%E3%83%
83%E3%82%AF%E3%83%A
2%E3%83%BC%E3%83%AB
/51f7cfcfd498e85998bdda981

YANESEN & NIPPORI

1 **Yanaka Senbei Shinsendo**

2 **Yanaka Ginza:**
yanakaginza.com/

3 **Hankoya Shinimonogurui:**
ito51.com/

4 **Yakikarintou:** yakikarinto.jp/

5 **Motherhouse:**
mother-house.jp/aboutus/

6 **Niku no Suzuki:**
tabelog.com/en/tokyo/A1311/
A131106/13022715/

7 **Atom bakery:**
atom-bakery.com/atom/

8 **Kanekichien:**
yanakaginza.com/shop/
kanekichien/

9 **Waguriya:** waguriya.com/
tokyo.html

10 **Yanesen Centre:** ti-yanesen.jp/

11 **Nezu Jinja (shrine):**
www.jnto.go.jp/eng/location/
spot/shritemp/nezujinja.html

12 **Asakura Choso:** taitocity.net/
taito/asakura/english/index.
html

13 **Kaizoin**

14 **Choanji Temple:**
www.choanji.net/index.html

15 **Kanoin**

16 **HAGISO:** hagiso.jp/

17 **Isetatsu:** isetatsu.com/

18 **Biscuit:** biscuit.co.jp/
webshop/

19 **Gate of Life**

20 **Antique Hatsune:**
antique-hatsune.com/

21 **Sankenma:**
taireki.com/sankenma/

22 **Kamitonuno:** kamitonuno.
com/index.html

23 **Craft Studio Tokugen:**
tokugen.co.jp/item/pg238.
html

24 **Scai the Bathhouse:**
scaithebathhouse.com/en/

25 **Shitamachi:**
taitocity.net/taito/
shitamachi/husetsu.html

26 **Inamura:**
inamura.jp/index.html

27 **Nippori Senigai**
(fabric street):
nippori-senigai.com

28 **Tokyo National Museum:**
tnm.jp

ACKNOWLEDGMENTS

Thank you, Japan, as always, for your exquisite hospitality.

Thank you, Tokyo city, and to all the patient folk and businesses who put up with me lingering in their establishments and whipping my camera around.

Thank you as always Murdoch Books for putting the stuff I write and photograph onto paper and turning it all into books. I so appreciate you allowing me to show off a little of my beloved adopted second home.

Particular thanks go to publishing boss lady Sue Hines, publisher Corinne Roberts, design manager Hugh Ford, designer Justin Thomas, editorial managers Katie Bosher and Barbara McClenahan, and editor Jen Taylor.

Thanks to my friends, family and colleagues for your help and support at various stages of this book—even if that was simply sharing a few meals, drinks and stories during my Tokyo research and shoot. Always fun to share a city with others! These treasures include: Gerard Kambeck, Katsuji Tochino, Daisuke Mizukoshi, Linh Saunderson, Mari Antoinette Mori, Brendhan Kelly, David Buchler, Koichi Tanabe, Bridget Scott and Tad McNulty. And finally, thanks to Yoshi and Meiko (RIP) for truly making us feel at home in your Tokyo. Meiko san—your beauty shines on. x

And Mum—my seed of interest in Japan would never have been allowed to germinate and grow had it not been for your eternal support (both emotional and financial!). Thank you, this book is a blossom on a truly nurtured branch. xx

Published in 2016 by Murdoch Books, an imprint of Allen & Unwin

Murdoch Books Australia
83 Alexander Street
Crows Nest NSW 2065
Phone: +61 (0)2 8425 0100
Fax: +61 (0)2 9906 2218
murdochbooks.com.au
info@murdochbooks.com.au

Murdoch Books UK
Ormond House
26–27 Boswell Street
London WC1N 3JZ
Phone: +44 (0) 20 8785 5995
murdochbooks.co.uk
info@murdochbooks.co.uk

For Corporate Orders & Custom Publishing, contact our Business Development Team
at salesenquiries@murdochbooks.com.au.

Publisher: Corinne Roberts
Editorial Managers: Barbara McClenahan and Katie Bosher
Design Manager: Hugh Ford
Design Concept: Justin Thomas
Editor: Jen Taylor
Production Managers: Alex Gonzalez and Rachel Walsh

A cataloguing-in-publication entry is available from the catalogue of the National
Library of Australia at nla.gov.au.

ISBN 978 1 74336 568 7 Australia
ISBN 978 1 74336 569 4 UK

A catalogue record for this book is available from the British Library.

Colour reproduction by Splitting Image Colour Studio Pty Ltd, Clayton, Victoria
Printed by 1010 Printing International Limited, China